www.tredition.de

AF204975

Robert Maschmann

The Survival of Mankind

Conjectures about the preconditions for the continued
existence of the animal species *Homo sapiens*

www.tredition.de

ISBN Softcover: 978-3-384-06068-6
ISBN Hardcover: 978-3-384-06069-3
ISBN E-Book: 978-3-384-06070-9

Printed and distributed on behalf of the author:
tredition GmbH, Heinz-Beusen-Stieg 5, 22926 Ahrensburg,
Germany

.

TABLE OF CONTENTS

1 Introduction

The IUCN Red List of Threatened Species (available at www.iucnredlist.org) is a globally recognized assessment and classification of biological species developed and maintained by the IUCN, the International Union for Conservation of Nature, and Natural Resources. It is an important reference source for the status and endangerment of animal, plant, and fungal species on a global level.

This Red List of Threatened Species uses different categories to describe the endangerment status of a species. The main categories range from

"Extinct (EX): The species no longer exists"

to

"Not Endangered (LC): A species not currently facing an imminent threat".

Extinction" is the final disappearance of a species or a group of organisms. A species is considered extinct when it no longer has any living individuals and reproduction is no longer possible. Extinction can be either local, when a species becomes extinct only in a certain area, or global, when the entire species becomes extinct on the entire planet.

The classification of a species in one of these Red List of Threatened Species categories is always based on scientific evidence about population trends, range, population size, threats, and other relevant factors. This Red List of Threatened Species is regularly updated to incorporate new information and to monitor the status of threatened species.

The IUCN itself is an international organization dedicated to nature conservation. The IUCN was founded in 1948 and has its headquarters in Gland, Switzerland. IUCN brings together governments, non-governmental organizations, scientists, and experts from a variety of fields to promote the conservation of the natural diversity of species and the sustainable use of natural resources. It is an influential voice in environmental protection and has considerable influence at both national and international levels.

However, if one searches this IUCN Red List of Threatened Species for the animal species *Homo sapiens*, then one will not find it.

Yes, of course, one might now object, that is perfectly clear. Man, or *Homo sapiens* cannot appear on this Red List of Threatened Species as an endangered animal species, because man is man and not an animal. That would be however (unfortunately) completely wrongly thought. From a biological point of view, *Homo sapiens* is just as much an animal species as *Canis lupus*, *Equus asinus* or *Neofelis nebulosa*.

"For evolutionary biology, humans are one animal species among many, with characteristics that can be explained as adaptations to past and present environmental conditions. [...] The fact that humans have abilities that are found only in

7

rudimentary form in other animals - language, art, and science, for example - contradicts this only at first glance. From a biological point of view, humans have unique characteristics - just as all other living beings are special and unique in their own special way" (Junker 2021; p. 7).

Humans in their existence as animals and as living beings are then classified (as everybody knows) in the biological systematics as specimens of the genus *Homo*. The animal species *Homo sapiens* is the only and last remaining (recent) species of the genus *Homo*. All other species of the Hominines (i.e., species of the genus *Homo*) have disappeared sooner or later in the course of human evolution.

"In general, it can be stated that during most of the hominin evolution, several related species coexisted in the same geographic regions, perhaps even in the same places. Thus, the traditional picture of human evolution as a ladder of stages from ape-like ancestors to present-day humans is not accurate. It is more like a tree with many branches, some of which belong only to the early period, others reaching almost to the present. Unusual, however, is the present situation, in which there is only one species - *Homo sapiens*" (Junker 2021; p. 29).

If humans had to be classified as an animal species in this Red List of Threatened Species, then only the category "Not Endangered (LC)" would be possible for them. However, the animal species *Homo sapiens* is (at least at the moment) so far away from a possible extinction that even the classification into the category "Not endangered" would be a disproportionate exaggeration. For a problem of Mankind is currently not so much the possibility that it could become annihilated, but rather the problem of an increasing overpopulation of Earth by more and more people.

The animal species *Homo sapiens* is nevertheless constantly inscribing itself, indirectly so to speak, on this Red List of Threatened Species. Because the animal species *Homo sapiens* is in the process of wiping out and causing the disappearance of other biological species on a grand scale through its uncontrolled reproduction in connection with the way it manages its planet, whereby this Red List of Threatened Species is becoming longer and longer.

But even though the animal species *Homo sapiens* would not even be classified as endangered with regard to its survival, at least from a scientific point of view, there are still people who fear that Mankind will not survive and that the animal species *Homo sapiens* could disappear from Earth forever. And many people who believe that the end of Mankind is possible could certainly put together a whole potpourri of catastrophes off the top of their heads that could wipe out Mankind. These would certainly include climate change, the nuclear threat, the proliferation of weapons of mass destruction, pandemics and other global health crises, and social, political, and economic instabilities. To name just a few of these possible catastrophes.

So, although on the one hand humans are by no means among the threatened animal species on this planet, on the other hand people are obviously (also) concerned and fearful that Mankind might not survive and thus the animal species *Homo sapiens* might be wiped out forever. This seems to be a contradiction.

In this book I will show that this apparent contradiction is not one. I will show that people's fear that Mankind could be wiped out in whatever way is undoubtedly well-founded and that this fear is thus not just the unfounded imagination of a species that is apparently permanently more or less so overwhelmed with its own existence that it therefore constantly fantasises its own demise.

If, however, this fear of people that Mankind could be wiped out by whatever events is actually justified, then a question immediately arises, the answer to which is, so to speak, the purpose of this book: What would be the preconditions that would have to be fulfilled so that under all possible circumstances and for every conceivable case this wiping out of Mankind could be prevented or avoided and so there would be no end of Mankind? In accordance with the subtitle of this book, I will therefore make speculations about the conditions under which the continued existence of the animal species *Homo sapiens* and thus also of Mankind could be guaranteed under all possible circumstances and for every conceivable case.

But this also means that the content of this book is more or less already mapped out.

First, I will try to determine what is meant by the term "Mankind" in the first place. Yes, it is true: The term "Mankind" is used all the time and everywhere, and above all when people want to emphasise the drama, the scope, the moral relevance and thus the importance of their findings, insights, and actions. As will be shown, a (meaningful) definition of the term "Mankind" is not so easy at first. In any case, however, it would be wrong to define the term "Mankind" in such a way that it simply denotes the people living now or today. For then the term "Mankind" would simply denote nothing and would only be an empty term.

Then I will discuss which experiences and insights can lead people to fear that Mankind might not survive. This is all the more astonishing because there is no experience of whether Mankind could be wiped out. For if people had already had some experience of the end of Mankind, then I would not exist, nor would any other human being, and this book here would never have been written. In this context, it will then also become apparent that, as I have already said, people's fears that all human beings could be wiped out by catastrophic events and that the history of Mankind could thus also come to an end are quite justified.

Then, after discussing what might usefully be meant by the concept of Mankind and why people may reasonably fear that Mankind will not survive and that the history of Mankind may come to an end at some point, I will determine, on the basis of the concept of Mankind I have developed, what conditions must be in place for it to be possible to say, at any point in the future and for any point in the future, that Mankind has survived and that the history of Mankind has not yet come to an end.

I will then set out to find events that could lead to the annihilation of Mankind, in order to determine, through the analysis of these events, the conditions that would have to exist in any case and under any circumstances for Mankind to survive such events and so that at any time in the future and for any time in the future it could be said that Mankind has survived and that the history of Mankind is not yet over. I distinguish between events on the planetary, cosmic, and cosmological levels.

If one goes in search of events that could endanger the survival of Mankind on the planetary level, then these are events that have their cause on Earth itself and could wipe out Mankind through their destructive potential. In this context, I will of course (must) also discuss the consequences of man-made climate change for the continued existence of Mankind. However, I can and will then give good reasons why man-made climate change does not and cannot mean the end of Mankind. It will also be shown that no single event on the planetary level would be capable of wiping out Mankind.

When one looks for events that could endanger the survival of Mankind on the cosmic level, then these are events that have their cause in the solar system or in outer space and that could, so to speak, cause the annihilation of Mankind from there. Certainly, the most prominent example of such an event is an asteroid which, due to its trajectory through the solar system, could hit Earth and cause such devastating damage that human life on Earth would no longer be possible. However, it will become apparent that it is not the asteroids flying around in the solar system that pose the greatest cosmic threat to Mankind. For there is a cosmic event that is certain to occur and which, if it did occur, would certainly wipe out Mankind. From this event one can then conclude very clearly which conditions would have to be fulfilled at least on the cosmic level in order to be able to avoid and prevent an annihilation of Mankind at least on this level.

If one goes in search of events that could endanger the survival of Mankind on the cosmological level, then on this level it is actually not a question of individual events that could occur, but of certain states that the universe as a universe itself could assume and that could cause the annihilation of Mankind because the universe could assume such a state that would make life and thus also human life impossible in this universe. The universe could (at least according to the conclusions of cosmologists as well as astrophysicists, which they draw from their equations, observations, and simulations) assume such a state in the course of time because the universe is not a static but a dynamic universe and changes and develops, so to speak, as a universe itself. If there could be such states of the universe that would make all life in the universe impossible, then one can likewise derive from these possible states of the universe those preconditions that would have to be fulfilled under all circumstances and in any case and without restriction on the cosmological level (so to speak on the level of the universe itself) so that Mankind could survive and would not become annihilated.

Finally, and at the very end, I will discuss the consequences for the survival of Mankind if it were possible to make people immortal.

So that no misunderstandings arise here: Of course, I am not referring to any kind of metaphysical concepts of immortality, such as the idea of an immortal human soul that survives the death of humans. I will refer to such assumptions as notions of some kind of **transcendent immortality**. I will call the idea of a transcendent immortality of human beings the idea that a human being could live on beyond death in an immaterial form of whatever kind. A human being becomes transcendently immortal when the body of this human being dies, but his soul, spirit, consciousness, or ego (or whatever other immaterial entities one might consider potentially immortal in the context of human existence) continue to exist practically forever beyond death. This transcendent immortality is of no importance for the survival of Mankind because transcendent immortality is a merely imagined immortality of people who have already died and are dead.

What is important for the survival of Mankind is that immortality which I will call **inner-worldly immortality**, for this inner-worldly immortality would be the immortality of living human beings and thus also the guarantee for the survival of Mankind. I will call the idea of inner-worldly immortality the idea that people could, on the one hand, achieve **biological immortality**, i.e., stop the ageing process of their bodies and achieve an unlimited regenerative capacity of their bodies. On the other hand, I understand inner-worldly immortality to be what I will call **machinic immortality**. The idea of machinic immortality is the idea that although a human body dies, its soul, spirit, consciousness, or ego could somehow be stored on or transferred to a non-human material substrate, and that human beings (at least any immaterial parts of them) could achieve immortality in this way.

This chapter on the possibility of an inner-worldly immortality of human beings and the consequences of such an inner-worldly immortality of human beings for the survival of Mankind is, however, already the conclusion of this book, because I will not pass judgement on whether Mankind can survive or will sooner or later be extinguished on the basis of the preconditions which I will then have established on the planetary, cosmic and cosmological levels for the survival of Mankind. Within the framework of this book, I see my task only in determining and presenting these preconditions on the basis of the scientific knowledge that we (i.e., human beings and Mankind) have accumulated so far about Earth, the cosmos and the universe. Everyone who reads this book and thinks about the preconditions I have tried to determine here with regard to the survival of Mankind, should make his own judgement as to whether Mankind can survive or whether it will inevitably become annihilated sooner or later.

Now up to this point I have always used the term "Mankind" as a matter of course and spoken of Mankind, which may not survive and whose history may come to an end. But what is that anyway: "Mankind"? What does the term "Mankind" mean? Are we talking about something specific at all when we use the term "Mankind"? In the following chapter I will try to answer these questions and develop a definition of the term "Mankind".

2 Mankind

I am sure that if you were to ask random people in a pedestrian zone in any city in the world what is meant by "Mankind", most people would answer that "Mankind" means the totality of all people who live on Earth or who exist on Earth. But, as I will show in a moment, this would not be a meaningful and useful definition of the term "Mankind". The simple reason for this is that this definition of the term "Mankind" is, on the one hand, too imprecise to be able to use it meaningfully, since this definition of Mankind does not specify a concrete point in time at which these people live on Earth and, on the other hand, is again too narrowly defined, because Mankind then consists, even if one specifies a certain point in time, not only of the people who live on Earth at this certain point in time, but also of the people who lived on Earth before this certain point in time and who will have lived on Earth after this point in time.

The statement that Mankind means all human beings who live or exist on Earth would only define the term "Mankind" correctly in its generality if all human beings who live on Earth had always been immortal inner-worldly and if they had never at any time begotten human beings. If the number of human beings on Earth were constant, because these human beings had always been immortal inner-worldly and at the same time had never begotten "new" human beings, then the human beings living today would be identical with the human beings living yesterday and also identical with the human beings living tomorrow, and then and only then would Mankind always be identical with the totality of human beings living on Earth.

The statement: "Mankind is the totality of all people living on Earth" would therefore only be correct in this generality if people had always been immortal inner-worldly and had never fathered children, because the quantity or totality of all living people is not constant and changes permanently, since people are constantly being born, but people are also constantly dying. At the moment, an average of about 4.3 people are born and about 1.8 people die every second worldwide. In this sense, Mankind is growing by about 2.5 people per second. Or by about 80 million people per year. The fact that the exact number of people born and died per year, per day or even per second cannot of course be determined exactly is not relevant for the definition of the term "Mankind". What is relevant for this definition is only that the number of living people is not constant and that this number changes permanently due to the birth and death of people. And this is indisputably so.

If one were to make the statement that Mankind is the totality of all people living on Earth, then, since the totality of people living on Earth is constantly changing, one must always specify a certain period of time within the framework of which the totality

of people living on Earth or who exist is to be determined.

If, for example, a speaker were then to preface her
statement: "Mankind is the totality of all people
who live on Earth." and say that Mankind consists
of the totality of all people who live on Earth today,
then she would also have to specify this "today"
once again by stating the exact time, which date is
actually meant by "today".

Thus, if by "today" (assumed) the speaker meant the
day 01.01.2023 from 00:00 o'clock to 24:00 o'clock,
one could then determine Mankind on the day
01.01.2023 and call the thus determined totality of
people who were alive on the day 01.01.2023 "Mankind on the day 01.01.2023". If one had wanted to
include the totality of all people who made up
Mankind on the day 01.01.2023, then one would
have had to wait until the day 01.01.2023 was over
and history, since until the end of the day 01.01.2023
the number of living people would have changed
constantly through death and above all through the
birth of people.

Therefore, it would only make sense to say that
Mankind on the day 01.01.2023 consists of the totality of all people who lived and existed on Earth during this day 01.01.2023, since it is only in retrospect
that one can survey the entire period of this day
01.01.2023 and thus also the number of people who
lived and existed on this day, since, to repeat, the
number of people who live and exist is constantly

changing due to the fact that people are born, but also people die. The totality of all people who would form Mankind on the day 01.01.2023 would then be the people who were alive and lived on Earth at the beginning of this day 01.01.2023 plus the approximately 216,000 people who during this day 01.01.2023 joined Mankind as "new" people, so to speak, through their birth. The people who were alive at the end of the day 01.01.2023 are then those people who form the totality of all people who are alive at the beginning of the day 02.01.2023. These are the people who were alive at the beginning of the day 01.01.2023 minus the approximately 155,520 people who died during the day 01.01.2023 and plus the approximately 371,520 people who were born on the day 01.01.2023. How do I arrive at these 216,000, 155,520 and 371,520 people? Quite simple.

The day 01.01.2023 has a total of 24 hours. These 24 hours have 1440 minutes, and these 1440 minutes have 86,400 seconds. If we take the average mortality rate of currently about 1.8 people per second, then about 155,520 people will have died on the day 01.01.2023. If we take the average birth rate of currently about 4.3 people per second, then on this day 01.01.2023 about 371,520 people will have been born. This means that on this day 01.01.2023 Mankind will have grown by about 216,000 people.

In order to clarify these relationships once again, I will construct a small model of Mankind at this point, in which I will determine that the total population of people on the day 01.01.2023 at 00:00

o'clock consists of the people P_1 to P_{1000}. Of these people P_1 to P_{1000}, the people P_1 to P_{10} are assumed to die in the period of the day 01.01.2023. At the same time, however, the people P_{1001} to P_{1022} are born in this period of the day 01.01.2023. On the day 01.01.2023 at 24:00 o'clock sharp, the total population of people then consisted of people P_{11} to P_{1022}. The number of people alive during this period has thus increased by 12 people during this period of the day 01.01.2023 from 00:00 o'clock to 24:00 o'clock as 10 people died and 22 people were born. It can be clearly seen that the composition of people living and existing in a given period is constantly changing due to the birth and death of people. Furthermore, the number of people also increases steadily over the course of this period, as more people are born than die.

The Mankind on the day 01.01.2023 at 00:00 o'clock consisted at this time of the people P_1 to P_{1000} and on the day 01.01.2023 at 24:00 o'clock at this time of the people P_{11} to P_{1022}. These people P_{11} to P_{1022} now form the total population of people on the day 02.01.2023 at 00:00 o'clock. Of these people P_{11} to P_{1022}, people P_{11} to P_{20} are assumed to die in the period of the day 02.01.2023. At the same time, however, people P_{1023} to P_{1044} are assumed to be born in this period of the day 02.01.2023. On the day 02.01.2023 at 24:00 o'clock, the total population of people then consists of the people P_{21} to P_{1044}, who in turn form the total population of people on the day 03.01.2023 at 00:00 o'clock. And so on.

If one considers the entire period of the day 01.01.2023 from 00:00 o'clock to 24:00 o'clock, then the totality of all people who were alive and existed in this period consists of the people P_1 to P_{1022}. These people P_1 to P_{1022} then form the Mankind on the day 01.01.2023. The Mankind on the day 02.01.2023 would then have consisted of the people P_{11} to P_{1044}, as these were the people who were alive and existed during the entire period of the day 02.01.2023. As can be seen, the term "Mankind" in this small model of Mankind denotes something different in relation to the day 01.01.2023 than in relation to the day 02.01.2023. This would of course also be the case if one were to determine the actual number of people who were alive and existed on the day 01.01.2023 and on the day 02.01.2023.

If, however, one was to determine only Mankind on the day 01.01.2023, as in the above example, then one would exclude from the determination of Mankind all those people who were still alive on the day 31.12.2022, but who were no longer alive at the beginning of the day 01.01.2023, but who would undisputedly have to be added to Mankind, since they existed as human beings.

The first problem that arises from the specification of a certain period of time for the determination of a totality of people who are then to be Mankind is that all those people would be excluded from the determination of Mankind who lived or were alive on Earth before and after this period of time but would have to be counted as part of Mankind because they existed as human beings.

However, a second problem also arises from the specification of a certain period of time for the determination of a totality and a set of people who are then supposed to be Mankind in this period of time. For if a speaker were always to specify an exact period of time to which this statement refers with the statement: "Mankind is the totality of all people living on Earth", then of course, as the above example has also shown, there would not be "the one Mankind", but as many Mankinds as totals of people could be determined who were alive in different periods of time. In principle and purely theoretically, this would then be an infinite number of Mankinds that could be determined by one speaker.

These two problems can now be solved quite easily. For it follows from what has been said so far that Mankind as the totality of all human beings who were alive in a certain period of time becomes all the larger, the larger the period of time that is then determined by the statement: "Mankind is the totality of all human beings who lived in a certain period of time". If one chooses the period of time large enough that one means by this statement, then it is obviously possible to determine the entire Mankind as the largest possible number and as the largest possible totality of all human beings who have ever been alive. I will refer to this Mankind in the following as the **"one entire Mankind"**. This one entire Mankind would therefore not only be Mankind related to a "today" or a day or a year but related to the period of time in which all human beings have lived who have ever been alive. And every single human being would then be a representative of this one entire Mankind just by existing.

If one assumes that human beings are mortal and will also remain mortal and that Mankind is thus subject to constant change in the course of time, then one can define the one entire Mankind that would be designated by the term "Mankind" as the totality of all human beings who have lived and existed in a period of time chosen to be so large that all human beings who have ever lived and existed are gathered together in this period of time.

This one entire Mankind would only be a self-contained set of human beings if Mankind were not to survive, and the history of Mankind were to come to an end at some point. If, however, Mankind did survive, then, on the assumption that human beings can never and will never attain inner-worldly immortality, the period of time that would have to be considered in order to comprehend the one entire Mankind as those human beings who have ever been alive would necessarily have no end and the quantity of human beings who would alto-gether form the one entire Mankind would be infi-nitely great. I will return to these connections when I try to determine what is meant by the survival of Mankind.

But if the one entire Mankind consists of all people who have ever been alive and existed, then the question immediately arises as to when the history of Mankind began. Or, in other words: When did the first modern human being live as the first specimen of the animal species *Homo sapiens* and thus found Mankind? No one can answer this question. But at some point, in the past, there must have been at least one specimen of the genus *Homo* that could have been called the first modern human and thus the first specimen of the animal species *Homo sapiens*.

Even if it is not possible to determine when the first specimen of the animal species *Homo sapiens* existed, at the moment it seems at least certain that modern humans originated in Africa about 300,000 years ago and spread from there all over the world.

"For 2.5 million years, the genus *Homo* has developed a very extraordinary biocultural diversity. This phenomenon can only be explained by the interaction of humans with environmental factors, such as living space, habitat, food, competition, or social environment. Modern humans originated in Africa about 15,000 generations ago and from here they spread to the whole world. Africa is the place of origin of our common biological, social, and cultural evolution and thus also the origin of our knowledge and value systems" (Schrenk 2019; p. 115).

However, it is (of course) not decisive for the determination of the prerequisites for the survival of Mankind that no one knows exactly when the history of modern man and thus also the history of Mankind began, because in connection with the prerequisites for the survival of Mankind, it is not so much the past of Mankind that is interesting (although this is also a very exciting topic), but first and foremost its future. More precisely: the survival of Mankind in a future of whatever kind.

So now that I have tried to determine what might usefully be described by the term "Mankind", in the following chapter I will try to show that people are justified by good reasons to believe that Mankind could become annihilated and that the animal species *Homo sapiens* could thus disappear from Earth forever.

3 The worst-case scenario of complete annihilation

If one were to ask random people in a pedestrian zone in any city in the world whether it would be possible that Mankind would not survive, then I am sure that the overwhelming majority of all those asked would answer that this could undoubtedly be the case. Now, obviously, it is only not completely absurd to be convinced that Mankind could not survive if there were not at least the reasonable and justifiable possibility that the whole of Mankind could be wiped out. So, the question is, what would be plausible reasons that these people could give for their conviction that it is indeed possible that Mankind will not survive?

However, these plausible reasons cannot trivially be derived from any kind of experience that people have had with the end of Mankind, since it is immediately obvious that there cannot possibly be any experience of people that it is possible that there will be an end of Mankind.

For it is obvious and undoubtedly true that the survival of Mankind will have failed at the latest when there are no more human beings at some point. Or to put it more directly: When all human beings without exception are dead. If the last human being is dead, then the history of the one entire Mankind is also over, because there are no more human beings who could testify to and continue the history of the one entire Mankind through their existence. If all human beings were dead, the one entire Mankind would not have survived for the reason that the one entire Mankind would then only consist of a finite amount of already dead human beings. The one entire Mankind is thus alive as long as there are people who are alive and who, through their existence, can testify to and represent and also continue the existence of the one entire Mankind.

Thus, assuming that all human beings are dead, if the survival of Mankind has failed, human beings can never know that the survival of Mankind can actually fail, because since all human beings would then be dead in this case, trivially in this case no human being can also determine that all human beings are dead, and the survival of Mankind can thus actually fail because it has failed. The survival of Mankind has therefore failed precisely when there is no longer a human being who could determine that the survival of Mankind has failed.

If the survival of Mankind fails and the history of Mankind ends with it, then this represents a singular and non-repeatable event about which people can neither know anything nor have had any experience. For either the survival of Mankind has not yet failed. Then there is also no experience of people about whether the survival of Mankind can actually fail. Or the survival of Mankind has failed. But then there is also no human being who could know or who could say that he or she has had the experience that the survival of Mankind can actually fail.

The assertion that there is a possibility that Mankind will not survive is a thesis that cannot be proven, since some human being would have to establish that it is true, but who would cease to exist precisely when this thesis proved to be true and would thus be true. And since there are still people (at least at the time I am writing these lines), there has trivially never been a time in the history of Mankind when there were no more people and Mankind would not have survived. People can therefore only ever assume that there will or could be a point in time when there are no more people and Mankind would not have survived. Nevertheless, it seems very plausible to many people that there is a possibility that Mankind will not survive, and that the history of Mankind could come to an end at some point.

The first answer to the question of why people can become convinced that there could be an end to Mankind is now quite simple: people learn sooner or later that all people who are alive and who are yet to be born, without exception, must die in whatever way and can be killed. This conviction of people with regard to the death of people and also with regard to their own death is not innate but must actually be learned and acquired by people.

"While some thinkers held that a human being could only come to the insight that he himself must die through experience, others maintained that there was an a priori and intuitive certainty of death, i.e., that even a human being who had never experienced the death of another living being would know that he would die one day. However, the findings of empirical developmental psychology in recent decades leave no doubt that knowledge of one's own mortality is not innate but acquired. Children gradually come to a full understanding of the concept of "death", and they must learn that all people, including themselves, will die" (Wittwer 2020; p. 8).

Although a person could assume that he is the first immortal human being to exist on Earth, he could not give a single plausible and rational reason for this conviction. Quite the contrary. He can perceive in himself, sooner or later, all the signs of ageing and physical decay that he has also perceived in other people before they died.

"Ever since humans have existed, they have been dying. So far, no exception to this banal rule can be discerned from a technical-historical perspective. Even from a serious medical and scientific point of view, there is no indication that this will change in the foreseeable future. Biological death is obviously - just like birth - an anthropological constant" (Schäfer 2015; p. 149).

Biological death marks the definitive end of a living being as a living being. Humans are then biologically dead when their vital functions have irreversibly (i.e., non-returnably) come to a standstill in whatever way or have been brought to a standstill in whatever way. These vital functions of humans as living beings and as animals, which come to an irreversible standstill in the case of biological death, can be determined as follows:

"Today, there is widespread agreement that life is the process in which certain organic bodies organise and maintain themselves by means of the so-called vital functions. Which and how many of these functions there are depends on the degree of complexity of the respective biological species. The human organism has five vital functions: control by the central nervous system, blood circulation, respiration, metabolism, and temperature regulation. Certain organs or organ systems correspond to these five functions, for example the lungs correspond to respiration" (Wittwer 2020; p. 14).

Through the cessation of vital functions, the inner structure, and the inner order of human beings as living beings and as animals begins to dissolve, until they then, as merely dead bodies, have irrevocably lost all the qualities that distinguished them as living beings.

From the experience that all human beings have died or been killed in whatever way up to now, one can draw the unavoidable conclusion that all human beings who are alive and who are yet to be born, without exception, must die in whatever way at some point and can be killed if (and this is the limiting condition that will have to be discussed in more detail) it is not possible to make human beings immortal inner-worldly.

Now, one can justifiably object that no one can know whether all human beings (i.e., those who are still alive as well as those who have not yet even been begotten and born) must necessarily die and can be killed in whatever way, since, as the Scottish philosopher David Hume (1711 - 1776) showed, there is no rationally justifiable argument for this.

"Can empirical universal statements be justified? So far, one could argue, following Hume, many people have died. But does it follow that all people living now and later must also die? Not necessarily. It is possible that the first immortal is already among us. Like all sceptical arguments, this argument cannot be refuted" (Wittwer 2020; p. 9).

David Hume was and is an important, perhaps the most important representative of empiricism. Empiricism is the philosophical position that all knowledge is based on experience. Empiricism emphasises the importance of sense perception and experience as a source of knowledge and argues that ideas and concepts people have about the world develop through direct observation and experience of the world. Empiricists argue that people have no innate ideas or knowledge, but that all knowledge is derived from experience and sense perception. They reject the idea that there are innate ideas in the mind that exist independently of experience.

In his work "An Enquiry Concerning Human Understanding" (cf. Hume 2016), Hume also deals with the problem of induction.

Hume argues that induction, i.e., the inference from individual cases to general laws, is not based on any firm logical foundations. He criticises the assumption that the future will be similar to the past and rejects the idea of a necessary connection between cause and effect.

Hume, as already mentioned, believes that people's knowledge of the world is always based on experience. Since people observe that certain events occur repeatedly, they assume that similar events will also occur in the future. However, according to Hume, this conclusion from the past to the future is not logically compelling. There is no rational justification for the future behaving in the same way as the past.

Hume argues that people's beliefs about causal connections are based on a habit, or a mental mechanism based on people's experiences. People become accustomed to the repeated observation of cause-effect connections but cannot draw a logically compelling conclusion from them.

Overall, Hume questions the validity of induction and emphasises the limited scope of human knowledge. His reflections on induction have led to ongoing discussions in philosophy and philosophy of science and still influence the debate on the problem of induction today.

However, in order to discuss the conditions that could guarantee the survival of Mankind in any case and under all circumstances, it is not necessary to know or assume that all human beings who are alive and who are yet to be born must necessarily die in whatever way and can be killed. It is sufficient to assume that it is possible that all human beings who are alive and who are yet to be born, without exception, must die and can be killed in whatever way. From the experience that so far, all human beings have died and been killed in whatever way, it is at least possible to deduce that all human beings who are alive and who are still being born must die and can be killed in whatever way without exception.

Just as it can be deduced from experience that there is a possibility that the Sun will rise again tomorrow because it has already risen many times and it is therefore possible that this process can repeat itself, although of course there is no necessity that the Sun will rise again tomorrow. From the experience that the Sun has risen, at least the possibility can be derived that the Sun can rise and thus possibly will rise again.

From this possibility that all humans who are alive and who are yet to be born must die and can be killed in whatever way without exception, the following scenario can be derived, which I will call **"the worst-case scenario of complete annihilation"** in the following:

If there is a possibility that all humans who are alive and who are yet to be born, without exception, must die in whatever way and can be killed, then catastrophic events affecting the entire Earth and all humans could possibly lead to this, that all humans without exception would be killed by the effects of such events, or that the effects of such events would at least kill so many humans that the surviving humans would no longer have the possibility to reproduce in whatever way and thus in this way the history of Mankind would come to an end and Mankind would thus also not have survived.

Why am I talking about **"catastrophic"** events here? The word "catastrophic" is used to describe events that cause widespread and serious destruction, damage, or loss. They are usually unforeseen or uncontrollable events that have a significant negative impact on people and the environment.

And why have I also used the term **"worst case"** here? This is also immediately obvious and easy to explain. A worst case always refers to the worst possible or most unfavourable case of a development or a scenario with the worst possible conditions or outcomes. A worst case is an assumption or prediction that represents the worst possible circumstances, problems or consequences of a particular situation or event.

The concept of worst case is used in a wide variety of fields to conduct risk analysis or make decisions by considering the most negative impacts or consequences of decisions and events. The concept of the worst case helps to identify potential problems, vulnerabilities, or risks and to develop strategies to deal with or counteract them.

With regard to the survival of Mankind, the worst-case scenario of complete annihilation serves to determine the conditions that are suitable for preventing or avoiding precisely this worst-case scenario of complete annihilation in any case and under all circumstances. With regard to the survival of Mankind, the question thus arises as to which preconditions would have to be in place so that the worst-case scenario of complete annihilation does not occur in any case and under any circumstances.

By identifying and considering the worst case for a given scenario, precautions can be taken, contingency plans developed, and measures taken to minimise potential damage or loss. Considering a worst case allows for a kind of anticipated mitigation and better preparation for adverse scenarios.

If one evaluates the end of the history of Mankind as an event that is not supposed to occur, then, if one also wants to view this event from another perspective, there is thus a **risk** that the worst-case scenario of complete annihilation will actually occur, if one understands the term "risk" to mean the greater or lesser probability of the occurrence of a future event that is not supposed to occur because this event itself or the consequences from this event are evaluated as disadvantageous.

The term "risk" thus refers to the greater or lesser probability of the occurrence of undesirable or harmful events or undesirable or harmful consequences from these events. The term "risk" thus includes both the probability of the occurrence of an undesirable event and the probability of potential effects or damage that may result from the occurrence of this undesirable event.

Risk assessment must always take into account various factors, such as the probability of an event occurring, the potential impact, the severity of the possible damage, the availability of protective measures and the ability of people to deal with the consequences.

The preconditions that could enable the survival of Mankind under all circumstances are thus the preconditions that could prevent this worst-case scenario of complete annihilation from occurring under all circumstances and that could thus completely eliminate the risk of this worst-case scenario of complete annihilation actually occurring.

In addition to their conviction that all human beings who are alive and who are still being born must die sooner or later by whatever means and can be killed, human beings must also have the conviction that there are events by which not only individual living beings can be killed, but which could possibly wipe out entire species or genera of living beings, so that the worst-case scenario of complete annihilation could also occur as a result of such events, in order to be able to have the fear, on the basis of this conviction, that Mankind could not survive.

To repeat: If the survival of Mankind should fail, then by whatever events and in whatever way all humans living at a certain time would have to be killed or by whatever events and in whatever way at least so many humans would have to be killed that in whatever way a reproduction of humans would no longer be possible. These events would then bring the history of Mankind to an end and the animal species *Homo sapiens* as well as the genus *Homo* would be extinct. As a reminder, the animal species *Homo sapiens* is the only remaining (recent) animal species of the genus *Homo*. If the animal species *Homo sapiens* were extinct, then the genus *Homo* would also be extinct.

But where do people get their conviction that such events actually exist that can wipe out entire animal species or genera of living beings and cause them to disappear?

This question is now also quite simple to answer: Humans are convinced that there are events that can wipe out entire animal species and genera of living beings because, on the one hand, humans know that there have already been such events in the history of Earth and in the history of life and, on the other hand, humans also know that, in the course of their biological evolution, they themselves have developed the intellectual abilities and technical possibilities to bring about such events themselves. The animal species *Homo sapiens* is thus the first animal species on this planet that, through biological evolution, has developed abilities through which it can extinguish itself as an animal species. If one had a penchant for irony and sarcasm, then the fact that *Homo sapiens* is the first animal species to have developed the abilities to extinguish itself could well lead one to the conviction that *Homo sapiens* would justifiably have earned the title "crown of creation" on that basis alone.

If such an event, or perhaps a combination of such events, were to lead to the worst-case scenario of complete annihilation, then one would also speak of the annihilation of Mankind or the extinction of the genus *Homo* or the animal species *Homo sapiens*. I had already briefly mentioned and defined the term "extinction" in the introduction. However, since the possibility of the extinction of animal species makes it understandable why people may fear that the animal species *Homo sapiens* could also become extinct, I would like to discuss the concept of extinction in more detail at this point. So, what exactly is meant by the term "extinction"?

"Extinction is when the last individual in a taxonomic group (e.g., a species, genus or family) dies" (MacLeod 2016; p. 9).

Or is killed. The term "taxonomy" refers to the branch of biology that deals with the classification of living organisms into systematic categories.

The term "extinction" thus refers to a development at the end of which a species or a group of organisms no longer exists and no longer has any living representatives. The extinction of an animal species occurs when all individuals of an animal species have died or when they are no longer able to successfully reproduce and produce offspring. Extinction can be due to natural causes, such as environmental changes, disasters, diseases, or competition with other species. It can also occur due to human activities such as habitat destruction, overhunting, overfishing, pollution, or climate change. The extinction of an animal species can have serious ecological consequences and massively affect biodiversity and the balance in ecosystems.

However, the extinction of animal species is not an exceptional event; such events take place all the time.

> "From the average duration of fossil species [...] it can be concluded with some confidence that the proportion of species alive today is less than one per cent of all species that have ever lived on Earth" (MacLeod 2016; p. 23).

In other words, it is estimated that more than 99% of all biological species that have ever lived on Earth are already extinct. So, the fact that a certain animal species becomes extinct is not the exception, but the rule. This also applies to the animal species *Homo sapiens*. If, from the point of view of evolutionary biology, everything goes according to plan, then the animal species *Homo sapiens* will sooner or later be wiped out by natural selection and disappear from the surface of Earth. But the animal species *Homo sapiens* is not supposed to follow its evolutionary course. The animal species *Homo sapiens* should survive.

Nevertheless, it is reasonable to conclude that, from an evolutionary-biological point of view, nothing unusual would happen with regard to the animal species *Homo sapiens* if it actually became extinct, because this is the fate of all animal species, and it would thus share the fate of all animal species. If the animal species *Homo sapiens* were to become extinct due to the consequences of man-made climate change, for example, then the animal species *Homo sapiens* would simply not have been able to adapt biologically and culturally to those environmental conditions that it itself created. But this would make the animal species *Homo sapiens* just another failed experiment of biological evolution among millions and billions of other failed experiments that biological evolution has conducted. However, I will explain in more detail below why I do not consider man-made climate change to be an event that can bring about the worst-case scenario of complete annihilation and thus the extinction of *Homo sapiens*.

In principle, a distinction is made between mass extinction and background extinction with regard to the extinction of biological species.

Mass extinctions in the past are characterised by the extinction of a considerable number of biological species within a geologically short period of time, because these species were unable to adapt to sudden changes in their environment.

"Can we somehow generalise the extraordinary and repeated records of mass extinctions on Earth? In any case, there is no common cause - different events can be attributed to asteroids, ice ages or strong volcanic activity. Nor can the ecological effects be generalised - mass extinctions could lead to different ecological outcomes, with changes in the ecosystem not directly reflecting the severity of the loss of species. What the events have in common is that the upheavals in the environment happened quickly, the speed of change was as important as the magnitude. If the environment changes slowly, populations can adapt to the circumstances, but if it happens quickly, this may not be possible, leaving only migration or extinction. Mass extinctions show temporary but profound changes in the environment triggered by mechanisms inside Earth or somewhere in our cosmic neighbourhood" (Knoll 2023; p. 171).

The largest mass extinction known today and meanwhile well researched occurred towards the end of the Permian, about 252 million years ago.

The Permian is a geological period that began about 298.9 million years ago and ended about 252.2 million years ago. It is the last period of the Palaeozoic Era and follows the Carboniferous. The Permian is named after the Permian region in Russia, where the rocks of this period were first extensively studied.

During the Permian there were significant changes on Earth, including the formation of the supercontinent Pangaea. The climate was largely arid and there were extensive deserts. The flora was diverse and included first flowering plants, ferns, and horsetails. The fauna was also diverse and included large amphibian-like reptiles, early mammal-like reptiles, and a variety of marine life.

The Permian ended with the largest mass extinction in Earth's history, the so-called Permian-Triassic mass extinction, which wiped out about 90% of marine biological species and 70% of terrestrial biological species. This event marks the end of the Palaeozoic and the beginning of the Mesozoic.

"At the turn of the 20th and 21st centuries, the Permian extinction event received increasing attention. This was mainly because it was the most devastating such event ever: according to an estimate frequently repeated today, up to 90 per cent of all biological species disappeared at that time" (Ward/Kirschvink 2018; p. 304).

In contrast to events of mass extinction of biological species, the so-called background extinction takes place continuously and evenly through natural selection due to a gradual change in the environment. However, these background extinction events have wiped out most of the biological species that have existed until now.

"Mass extinction events are regarded by most researchers as extraordinary phenomena that require extraordinary explanations. As a result, background extinctions are often associated with extinctions that occur through the normal Darwinian evolutionary process of competition and natural selection. However, looking at the raw numbers, background extinctions are much more significant. It is estimated that more than 95 per cent of all species extinctions in the history of life occurred during intervals of background extinction. This fact alone makes background extinction an important, though strangely often overlooked, category in the history of extinction" (MacLeod 2016; p. 56).

Whether caused by events that cause a mass extinction or by events that cause a gradual background extinction: Humans know that in the course of time animal species can become extinct and that in the course of biological evolution and the history of Earth countless animal species have already become extinct and that this can in principle and without doubt also affect the animal species *Homo sapiens*.

In summary, the question can now be answered as to why people can have the justified conviction that there is a possibility that Mankind will not survive, and that the worst-case scenario of complete annihilation could occur:

1. On the one hand, people learn that all human beings are living beings who sooner or later have to die in whatever way and can be killed. People learn that the existence of all human beings ends sooner or later with biological death. The fact that people have the justified conviction that all human beings without exception must die sooner or later in whatever way and can be killed is one prerequisite for people also being able to have the justified conviction that it is possible that in the worst case the entire animal species *Homo sapiens* can be annihilated and thus the possibility exists that Mankind will not survive.

2. On the other hand, humans know that they are an animal species that can become extinct, since it is not the exception but the rule in evolutionary biology that animal species become extinct and disappear from the surface of Earth again over time. Humans know that there are events that can lead not only to individual specimens of an animal species being killed off, but that can lead to an entire animal species, and thus

possibly the entire animal species *Homo sapiens*, being annihilated. The best known (but not the most devastating) extinction event in this context is probably the extinction of the dinosaurs at the end of the Cretaceous period about 66 million years ago. Knowledge of these events is the second prerequisite for people to have the justified conviction that there is a possibility that Mankind might not survive, and that the history of Mankind might end.

In the next chapter, I will now try to determine what conditions must exist so that at any given time and for any given time in the future it can be said that Mankind has survived and that the history of Mankind has not yet come to an end, in order to then set out on a search for events on the planetary, cosmic and cosmological levels that could lead to the annihilation of Mankind, and then, by analysing these events, to determine the conditions that would have to exist in any case and under any circumstances for Mankind to survive such events and for it to be possible to say at any time and for any time in the future that Mankind has survived and that the history of Mankind is not yet over.

4 The survival of Mankind

Following the above definition of Mankind, one can now define that Mankind survives or would have survived if, from a certain point in time T_n, at which at least one living human being exists or has existed as a specimen of the animal species *Homo sapiens*, at any point in time T_x after this certain point in time T_n, at least one living human being exists as a specimen of the animal species *Homo sapiens*.

Conversely: If at any time T_x after a certain time T_n, at which at least one living human being exists or has existed as a specimen of the animal species *Homo sapiens*, no living human being exists (anymore) as a specimen of the animal species *Homo sapiens*, then Mankind would not have survived. And then, as already mentioned, the period of time that one would have to consider in order to grasp the one entire Mankind as the totality of all human beings who have ever been alive would also be finite, since from a certain point in time there would then no longer be a living human being. Then the quantity of people who would form the one entire Mankind would also be a finite quantity of people and this quantity of people who would form the one entire Mankind would only be a quantity of already dead people. Since in this case the one entire Mankind would only consist of dead people, in this sense Mankind would not have survived.

This also makes it immediately apparent that the survival of Mankind, viewed from any point in time T_n at which at least one living human being exists or has existed as a specimen of the animal species *Homo sapiens*, requires an unlimited and never-ending future after this arbitrary point in time T_n.

After any arbitrary time, T_n, at which at least one living human being exists or has existed as a specimen of the animal species *Homo sapiens*, there must be an infinite number of other arbitrary times T_m. Or, in other words: time must not end, and the future must be unlimited and infinite, so that in this infinite and unlimited future an infinite number of people can exist continuously one after the other. (This would also apply if human beings were immortal: Immortal humans would also have to exist continuously forever for Mankind to survive. Therefore, time must not end for immortal humans either, since an infinite duration of time is precisely one of the conditions of the possibility of immortality).

For if, from a certain point in time T_n, at which at least one living human being exists or has existed as a specimen of the animal species *Homo sapiens*, the future (and thus time) would end after this point in time T_n at a certain point in time T_m, then the history of Mankind would also inevitably end at this point in time T_m and Mankind would not have survived, because from this point in time T_m onwards there would no longer be a living human being as a specimen of the animal species *Homo sapiens*. Since humans live in a universe in which space and time form a unity (which is why one cannot go to the same place twice) and (also) humans embody this space-time, in order for Mankind to survive, there must be an eternal space-time in the form that the existence of the animal species *Homo sapiens* in the form of individual specimens as moments of this space-time is possible at least theoretically (insofar as the worst-case scenario of complete annihilation does not occur) for all eternity.

If one assumes that human beings are not immortal and do not become immortal, then, as already mentioned, Mankind, if it were to survive, would have to consist of an infinite number of human beings. The reason for this is that human beings only have a limited lifespan and thus, with their limited existence and their limited lifespan, would always have to continuously embody the presupposed infinite and unlimited space-time (viewed from a certain point in time T_n at which at least one living human being exists or has existed as a specimen of the animal species *Homo sapiens*) with at least one human being as a specimen of the animal species *Homo sapiens*.

But how can the survival of Mankind now be ensured when, as has been shown, there could undoubtedly be events that could bring about the worst-case scenario of complete annihilation and thus endanger the survival of Mankind, and which could thus lead to, that from a point in time T_n at which at least one living human being exists or has existed as a specimen of the animal species *Homo sapiens*, there could be a point in time T_x in a more or less distant future at this point in time T_n at which no living human being would exist as a specimen of the animal species *Homo sapiens* anymore? Quite simply: from the analysis of such events, it would be possible to reliably derive the conditions that would have to be met so that the worst-case scenario of complete annihilation could not occur under any circumstances as a result of these events. In this context, only those events are of interest (of course) that could occur according to the current state of scientific research (but do not necessarily have to occur) and that could also have the destructive potential according to the current state of scientific research, either as a singular event or in combination with other events, to bring about the worst-case scenario of complete annihilation.

Thus, in the search for the conditions that could guarantee the survival of Mankind in any case and under all circumstances, one must look more closely at such events that

a) could occur according to the current state of scientific and, in particular, physical knowledge and which, if they do occur,

b) as a single event or in combination with other events, could bring about the worst-case scenario of complete annihilation in order to then

c) to be able to determine, on the basis of these events, the conditions which, in view of such possible events, could in any case and under any circumstances ensure the survival of Mankind.

In the following three chapters I will now set out to find such events on a planetary, on a cosmic as well as on a cosmological level and, should I find such events, discuss the preconditions that would have to be in place for Mankind to survive despite the catastrophic consequences from these events.

4.1   The planetary level

If one is looking for events that could cause the worst-case scenario of complete annihilation on the planetary level, then one cannot avoid a discussion of man-made climate change. For the sake of clarity, I am of course speaking here of man-made climate change, since there is also climate change that is permanently taking place on Earth due to a wide variety of causes that have nothing to do with human activity. Human-induced climate change is therefore climate change that is caused by the fact that since the beginning of the industrial revolution, humans have released enormous quantities of greenhouse gases into the atmosphere, which cause or have caused a sharp increase in the average temperature on Earth within a very short period of time in the history of Earth. According to the models of climate scientists (depending on the model), this man-made climate change could cause such drastic changes to and in the planetary ecosystems that modern industrial and technical civilisation could collapse. Stefan Rahmstorf, a well-known German climate researcher, for example, writes about a world in which the average global temperature is 3 degrees higher than it is now:

"No one can say exactly what this world would look like - it would be too far outside the experience of human history. But almost certainly this Earth would be full of horrors for the people who would have to experience it. Weather chaos with deadly heat waves, devastating monster storms and persistent widespread droughts that could trigger global hunger crises. Rising sea levels that devastate our coasts. Tilting ecosystems, devastating animal species extinctions, burning and withering forests, acidified oceans. Failed states, huge numbers of people fleeing. [...] I am not sure whether the halfway civilised coexistence of people as I know it will last. Personally, I consider a 3-degree world to be an existential threat to human civilisation" (Rahmstorf 2022; p. 29f).

In other words, man-made climate change can also be understood and interpreted as an event capable of bringing about the worst-case scenario of complete annihilation.

However, man-made climate change does not have the potential to actually bring about the worst-case scenario of complete annihilation. This lack of potential of man-made climate change to cause the annihilation of Mankind has, at least in my view, two main reasons:

1. On the one hand, descriptions of the consequences of man-made climate change usually convey the image that the entire Earth could become uninhabitable for human life as a result of these consequences of man-made climate change. The above quote from Stefan Rahmstorf is the best evidence of this. But this is not the case. Man-made climate change is not a global catastrophe but causes many local catastrophes. Human-induced climate change thus does not cause global devastation (such as the impact of a large asteroid), so that human life would no longer be possible on Earth.

2. On the other hand, man-made climate change is man-made. This means that the enrichment of Earth's atmosphere with greenhouse gases by humans would have reached its peak at the latest when the catastrophic consequences of man-made climate change had killed so many people that the emission of greenhouse gases caused by humans would be drastically reduced. Assuming that the catastrophic consequences of man-made climate change would leave only an average of 5% of the current world population alive in 2100. Thus, assuming the current world population of about 8 billion people, an average of about 400 million people would still make up the world population in 2100. These remaining 400 million people correspond to the average size of the world population at the beginning of the modern era, i.e., the

world population about 500 years ago. However, no one will claim that Mankind was on the verge of extinction in the year 1500, because the size of the world population at that time was "only" 400 million people and these 400 million people had not yet developed a modern industrial and technical civilisation. However, these remaining 400 million people in 2100 would, as already mentioned, would only produce a fraction of the greenhouse gases for their energy supply that today's world population produces. An enrichment of the atmosphere with greenhouse gases would then no longer take place and global warming would come to a halt (albeit probably at a high level) over the short term, but more likely over the long term. Under no circumstances, however, would man-made climate change cause Earth to heat up to such an extent that human life on Earth would no longer be possible. Man-made climate change would thus sooner or later come to a standstill by itself, without Mankind becoming extinct or having to become extinct as a result. These 400 million people (to return to the above example) would then (it can be assumed) populate those areas of Earth that would still be inhabitable or would be inhabitable again despite and perhaps precisely because of man-made climate change. And these 400 million people, and thus also Mankind, would not be threatened with extinction under any circumstances, since these people would be able to fall back on the remnants of the technical and industrial civilisation that, it is assumed, would have collapsed due to the catastrophic consequences of man-made climate change.

In many discussions about man-made climate change, prophecies, and speculations about the end of Mankind due to man-made climate change are very quickly at hand (at least that is my impression). Such invocations of the demise of Mankind are obviously intended to demonstrate in no uncertain terms the need to prevent man-made climate change by all means. However, when talking about the end of Mankind through man-made climate change, one should always keep in mind two facts that also apply to all other events that could bring about the worst-case scenario of complete annihilation on the planetary level:

1. Biological evolution has produced *Homo sapiens*, an animal species that (compared to other animal species) is extremely adaptable to the most diverse environmental conditions through the use of all kinds of techniques. Humans can survive in the most diverse environments under the most adverse conditions (and even in space). This is why they have colonised (one could also say conquered) the entire Earth within a very short evolutionary period. Humans survived, for example, even under the environmental conditions of the last ice age in Europe, which from today's point of view were

partly catastrophic, without the aids of technical and industrial civilisation.

2. The animal species *Homo sapiens* consists of an enormous quantity of specimens distributed over the entire Earth. In any case, it would have to be a devastating global catastrophe (which man-made climate change is not) that could kill off so many people (for which the potential of man-made climate change is not sufficient) that further reproduction (by whatever means) of the remaining specimens of *Homo sapiens* would be impossible, or that could even kill off all specimens of *Homo sapiens* within a very short time, so that the worst-case scenario of complete annihilation would become reality. But even if not 95%, but even 99% of the world's population of currently 8 billion people on average were to be wiped out by a global catastrophe, there would still be 80 million (!) people left who could ensure the continued existence of *Homo sapiens* through their enormous adaptability to the most diverse and adverse environmental conditions.

One cannot justify the measures that should be taken to stop man-made climate change on the grounds that otherwise Mankind would not survive. Man-made climate change certainly has the potential to kill millions or even billions of people. And perhaps you, as the person reading these lines right now, and I, as the person writing these lines right now, are also among those millions and billions of people. But man-made climate change just does not have the potential to bring about the worst-case scenario of complete annihilation.

Now, on the planetary level, in addition to man-made climate change, one encounters events of which one can certainly assume, and of which it is also undisputedly assumed, that they have the potential to bring about the worst-case scenario of complete annihilation, if they do occur. This applies, for example, to a **pandemic** or the formation of a **large igneous province** or the eruption of a **super-volcano**. What exactly is meant by such events and in what form could these events cause the worst-case scenario of complete annihilation?

A **pandemic** (in case it has perhaps already been forgotten) is the worldwide spread of a contagious disease across several countries or continents. A pandemic occurs when an infectious disease spreads rapidly and infects a significant quantity of people. Generally, a pandemic affects large populations and, as has been observed, has a severe impact on public health, the economy and society as a whole.

As everyone knows by now, a pandemic can have various causes, including viruses, bacteria, or other pathogenic microorganisms. Pandemics can spread through direct person-to-person contact, droplet infection or contact with contaminated surfaces.

However, a pandemic alone does not have the potential to destroy all of Mankind. Historically, pandemics have caused considerable loss of life, but Mankind has always recovered from them over time. This also confirms my thesis formulated above that the animal species *Homo sapiens* is such an enormously resilient and also adaptable species that it can survive even major global catastrophes, if not unscathed, but nevertheless without doubt. There is no doubt that a particularly severe pandemic can have a major impact on societies, economies, and global stability. A highly contagious disease with a high mortality rate, for which no effective treatment or vaccination is available, can lead to mass deaths and place a large or even too large burden on all health systems. This can lead to significant socio-economic dislocation and even destabilise the entire world order. But a pandemic alone does not have the potential to bring about the worst-case scenario of complete annihilation.

A **large igneous province**, also known as an igneous province, is an extensive geological region that has been formed or is being formed by the massive intrusion of magmatic material into Earth's crust and, as a consequence, by volcanic eruptions that have lasted for thousands of years. These provinces consist of a variety of magmatites, including intrusions of magma into Earth's crust and large amounts of volcanic rock.

Magmatites are igneous rocks that are formed by the solidification of magma. Magma, as everyone also knows, is a molten mass of rock that forms deep below Earth's surface and consists of molten rock, gaseous components, and minerals. Unlike magma, lava is molten rock that emerges from Earth's interior. Lava is formed when magma reaches Earth's surface. Lava usually emerges from volcanoes or fissures in Earth's crust during volcanic eruptions.

An **intrusion** is a geological process in which molten rock, i.e., magma, penetrates the solid rock layers of Earth's crust.

Large igneous provinces usually form in areas where there is increased magmatic activity, such as rift zones, subduction zones or hotspots.

A **rift zone** is a linear geological structure that forms in Earth's crust when lithospheric plates move apart. It is an area of increased geological activity characterised by volcanic activity, earthquakes, and the formation of new oceanic crust.

A **lithospheric plate**, also called a tectonic plate or Earth plate, is a large, fragmented block of Earth's outer rigid shell called the lithosphere. The **lithosphere** comprises all of Earth's crust and part of the upper mantle. These lithospheric plates move relative to each other.

A well-known example of a rift zone is the East African Rift Valley, which extends through East Africa and is an extension of the Great African Rift Valley. Active rifting is taking place here, and numerous volcanoes and lakes have formed. Somewhat strikingly, one could say that Africa is breaking apart at this point. Another example is the Mid-Atlantic

Ridge, which stretches across the Atlantic Ocean and whose tectonic activity is moving North America and Europe/Asia away from each other.

A **subduction zone** is an area where one lithospheric plate dips below another plate and is subducted into Earth's mantle. Subduction zones occur at convergent plate margins where two lithospheric plates meet and interact with each other. Probably the best-known result of the subduction of two lithospheric plates is the Mariana Trench in the western Pacific Ocean.

This is because the Mariana Trench was formed by tectonic activity at a subduction zone where two tectonic plates meet. In this case, it is the Pacific Plate dipping under the Philippine Plate.

The formation of the Mariana Trench began millions of years ago when the Pacific Plate slid under the Philippine Plate. This process is called subduction. As the Pacific Plate plunged under the Philippine Plate, a deep pit or gully formed along the subduction zone. This gully is the Mariana Trench.

The Mariana Trench is, incidentally, the deepest point on Earth and stretches over a length of about 2,550 kilometres. At its deepest point, the so-called "Challenger Deep", the trench reaches a depth of about 11,034 metres. This extreme difference in depth is the result of the collision and subduction of tectonic plates.

A **hotspot** is a geological region on Earth's surface within which magma rises from the mantle and causes volcanic activity independent of lithospheric plate movements. Unlike most volcanoes, which occur at the edges of tectonic plates, hotspots are located in the middle of a lithospheric plate.

Probably the best-known result of a hotspot is the archipelago of Hawaii in the Pacific Ocean. This is because the formation of Hawaii can be traced back to such a hotspot. In the case of Hawaii, this hotspot lies relatively stationary under the Pacific Plate. As the oceanic plate moves over the hotspot, the rising magma breaks through Earth's crust and leads to the formation of volcanoes.

As the oceanic plate continuously moves across the hotspot, different volcanoes were formed one after the other, which now together form the archipelago of Hawaii. The oldest volcanoes are at the north-western end of the archipelago, while the youngest are in the southeast.

The volcanic eruptions due to the hotspot resulted in deposits of ash and volcanic rock that gradually grew into islands. Each volcano in Hawaii essentially created its own island, and over time the entire archipelago of Hawaii formed.

This increased magma activity in rift zones, subduction zones or hotspots can lead to the formation of large magma chambers in the subsurface from which the magma rises into Earth's crust. The magmatic events that can then be caused by these large magma chambers at rift zones, subduction zones and hotspots, and which then form the large igneous provinces, can take place over a period of several million years. The resulting erupted lavas and intruded magmas can reach enormous extents and cover large geographical areas. Large igneous provinces are thus huge volcanic areas in which large quantities of lava and volcanic gases are released. Examples of large igneous provinces are the Deccan Trap in India, the Siberian Trap Province in Russia, and the Columbia River Basalt Group in North America.

The formation of large igneous provinces is accompanied by massive volcanic eruptions, lava flows and pyroclastic flows.

A **pyroclastic flow** is a high-energy, dense mixture of hot ash, volcanic gases and rock fragments that are ejected explosively during a volcanic eruption. Pyroclastic flows are extremely dangerous and can move down the slope of a volcano at high speed, unleashing great destructive power.

Pyroclastic flows occur when large quantities of volcanic ash, rock fragments and gaseous materials, such as water vapour and carbon dioxide, are ejected into the atmosphere during a volcanic eruption. Due to their density, these materials initially fall back onto the volcanic slope. However, due to the heat and pressure of the eruption, they are stirred up and form a turbulent, dense cloud that moves down the slope of the volcano at high speed.

Pyroclastic flows can reach temperatures of several hundred degrees Celsius and often travel at speeds of several hundred kilometres per hour. They have enormous destructive power and can destroy everything in their path. The heat and toxic gases of a pyroclastic flow make it one of the deadliest hazards in volcanic eruptions.

So, while the scale and consequences of the emergence of large igneous provinces could be significant regionally, the impact on Mankind as a whole would be limited. The emergence of large igneous provinces alone does not have the potential to destroy Mankind. Nevertheless, massive volcanic eruptions can have significant global consequences through their impact on the climate. Large quantities of volcanic gases and ash released into the atmosphere, as in the formation of large igneous provinces, can block solar radiation and lead to a temporary cooling of the climate.

There is also currently an almost unanimous opinion among palaeontologists that the impact of the so-called Chicxulub asteroid, which was the size of Mount Everest, combined with the formation of the large igneous provinces of the Deccan Traps about 66 million years ago, led to the extinction of the dinosaurs.

The Chicxulub asteroid got its name from the village of Chicxulub Pueblo on the Yucatán Peninsula in Mexico, under which the approximate centre of Chicxulub Crater is located.

This rock from space, which is said to be partly responsible for the extinction of the dinosaurs, is sometimes called the Chicxulub asteroid on the one hand and the Chicxulub meteorite on the other hand. In principle, however, both mean the same thing. This becomes clear when one looks at the difference or the similarities between an asteroid and a meteorite. Since these two terms come up again when discussing the events that could cause the worst-case scenario of complete annihilation on the cosmic level, I will explain them in more detail here in a moment.

Asteroids are small celestial bodies located mainly in the asteroid belt, a region between the planets Mars and Jupiter. Asteroids are remnants from the early phase of the formation of the solar system about 4.6 billion years ago. They are mainly made of rock and metal and can range in size from a few metres to hundreds of kilometres in diameter. Asteroids move in elliptical or roughly circular orbits around the Sun. Although the majority of asteroids are located in the asteroid belt, there are also those found in other parts of the solar system, including so-called Near-Earth Asteroids (NEAs), which can come close to Earth's orbit. Some asteroids have an orbit around the Sun that is close enough to Earth to be classified as potentially dangerous, since the impact of a larger asteroid on Earth can cause considerable (global) damage, as already mentioned.

A **meteorite** is a rock fragment or solid body made of an iron-nickel alloy that originates from space and has reached Earth's surface. Meteorites are the remains of asteroids, comets or other celestial bodies that pass-through Earth's atmosphere and are exposed to the heat and pressure during their entry into Earth's atmosphere, but do not burn up completely in Earth's atmosphere. An asteroid thus becomes a meteorite if it is large enough that, coming from space, it is not completely destroyed during its flight through Earth's atmosphere but hits Earth's surface.

So about 66 million years ago, an asteroid with a diameter of about 10 kilometres hit Earth. The impact of this Chicxulub asteroid released enormous amounts of energy. It is assumed that the impact triggered a devastating fireball explosion as well as massive fires, earthquakes, and tsunamis.

The impact of this Chicxulub asteroid had far-reaching global effects. It is believed that the meteorite impact filled the sky with dust and debris, resulting in a significant attenuation of Sunlight. This in turn had a dramatic effect on the climate with a significant cooling of temperatures. It is further believed that this led to a massive loss of plant biomass and ultimately the extinction of many animal species, including dinosaurs.

The Deccan Trap, on the other hand, also known as the Deccan Volcanic Province or Deccan Triassic Volcanic Province, is a vast volcanic region in the centre of India. It is one of the largest volcanic provinces in the world, covering an area of about 500,000 square kilometres.

The Deccan trap was formed by massive volcanic activity about 60 to 68 million years ago during the late Cenozoic. It is assumed that the eruptions took place over a period of several hundred thousand years and released an enormous amount of lava. The lava solidified into layers of volcanic rock known as traps.

The trap rocks of the Deccan Trap consist mainly of basalt, a dark, volcanic rock. The individual basalt flows of the traps extend over great distances and have an average thickness of several hundred metres.

The formation of the Deccan Trap had both geological and climatic impacts. Geologically, it has shaped the landscape of the Deccan Plateau, creating deep gorges and valleys. Climatically, the gases emitted, and the release of carbon dioxide may have led to short-lived (on a geological scale) but severe climate changes.

For this reason, the formation of the Deccan Trap is associated with the extinction of the dinosaurs at the end of the Cretaceous period. It is assumed that the massive release of sulphur dioxide and other gases during the eruptions led to climate change, which, in conjunction with the impact of the Chicxulub asteroid, contributed to the extinction of many animal species, including the dinosaurs.

But even these events did not lead to Earth becoming uninhabitable and life on it no longer possible, because otherwise obviously you, as the human being reading these lines right now, and also, I, as the human being writing these lines right now, would not be here and all the other living beings with us would not be here either.

There is no doubt that the emergence of large igneous provinces can lead to massive crop failures, global food shortages and severe ecological disruption, which can certainly lead to the death of millions or billions of people. But it is not particularly likely that the emergence of large igneous provinces will lead to the worst-case scenario of complete annihilation.

A **supervolcano**, on the other hand, is a volcano that is significantly larger and more explosive than conventional volcanoes. A supervolcano has the potential to release massive amounts of volcanic ash, rock and gas and can thus have much more catastrophic effects on the environment and human civilisation than conventional volcanoes.

Unlike conventional volcanoes, which typically form cone-shaped mountains, supervolcanoes are characterised by large, flat calderas. A caldera is a large, funnel-shaped depression formed by the collapse of a volcanic crater after a large volcanic eruption or explosive eruption has occurred. It is a special type of volcanic crater that is formed by the collapse of the upper part of the volcano, rather than by the build-up of volcanic material. A caldera can vary in diameter, from a few kilometres to dozens of kilometres. It is often surrounded by steep walls and can be filled with water, which then forms a so-called crater lake. A caldera can also be dry and filled with sediment or volcanic rock.

Examples of supervolcano calderas are the Yellowstone caldera system in the USA, Lake Toba in Indonesia, and the Campi Flegrei in Italy.

The eruption of a supervolcano can, as already mentioned, have catastrophic consequences. Enormous amounts of volcanic ash, rock and gas are released into the atmosphere, which can have far-reaching effects on the climate. The ash clouds can spread over great distances and block the Sun's rays, leading to a cooling of Earth's surface and possibly global cooling. The eruption can also produce pyroclastic flows that stream away from the volcano at high speed, destroying everything in their path.

Because of their enormous destructive potential, supervolcanoes are considered one of the greatest natural threats to Mankind. Fortunately, supervolcano eruptions are extremely rare and occur only once every hundred thousand or even million years. Nevertheless, supervolcanoes are constantly monitored and researched to gain a better understanding of their formation, eruption mechanism and potential impact, and also to predict the imminent eruption of a supervolcano.

For example, the eruption of a super-volcano like the eruption of Yellowstone in the USA or the eruption of the Phlegraean Fields in Italy would be devastating and a global catastrophe, but whether such an eruption could bring about the worst-case scenario of complete annihilation is very doubtful. It cannot be ruled out, but the eruption of a supervolcano does not necessarily cause the worst-case scenario of complete annihilation.

If we look at the planetary level, we can find events with an enormous destructive potential which, according to the current state of scientific knowledge, could also occur with a greater or lesser degree of probability in the near or distant future, but which, if they did occur, would very probably not have the destructive potential, at least as individual events, to bring about the worst-case scenario of complete annihilation. Thus, on the planetary level, no event can be found of which one could say that it would necessarily bring about the end of Mankind, because it will occur with necessity and because it would then necessarily bring about the worst-case scenario of complete annihilation due to its destructive power.

But nevertheless, in order to discuss which preconditions would also have to be in place on the planetary level so that humans could prevent the worst-case scenario of complete annihilation from occurring, I will assume the following scenario:

By a coincidence of unfortunate circumstances (whatever they may be), two of the perhaps 20 supervolcanoes on Earth erupt simultaneously and the eruptions of these supervolcanoes together have such a destructive potential that they can bring about the worst-case scenario of complete annihilation. The eruption of these supervolcanoes would therefore mean the definitive end of Mankind, because after these eruptions, sooner or later at least human life on Earth would be impossible. The question of what measures humans would have had to take in this case before this event occurred, in order to prevent this event or to escape the literally fatal consequences of this event, can now be answered relatively simply:

a) Before the eruptions of these supervolcanoes, humans would have had to have developed their technical capabilities and possibilities in such a way that it would have been possible for them not only to predict the eruptions of these supervolcanoes in whatever way, but also to prevent them.

If this were not successful, however, there would still be another possibility:

b) Before the eruptions of these supervolcanoes, humans would have had to have developed such technical capabilities and expanded and developed their technical possibilities in such a way that, in this case of the eruption of the supervolcanoes, they would have been able to evacuate at least so many people from Earth that the continued existence of Mankind would have been guaranteed despite the possibility of the worst-case scenario of complete annihilation.

No one can answer the question of how the eruption of one or more supervolcanoes could be prevented. At the present state of science and technology, there is no way to prevent or control the eruption of a supervolcano. The control or manipulation of such a huge and complex system is currently beyond the scientific and technological capabilities of humans. Perhaps in the distant future it will be possible. At the moment, however, there are not even any ideas about how it might be possible to prevent the eruption of a supervolcano.

However, a little more can be said about the evacuation of humans from Earth. The evacuation of humans from Earth is currently at least conceivable in that humans could build spaceships with which they could evacuate so many humans from Earth that the continued existence of Mankind would be assured and in which these humans could survive at least in the vicinity of Earth until the atmosphere, the lithosphere and the biosphere of Earth had recovered from the eruptions of these two supervolcanoes to such an extent that humans could repopulate Earth.

At first glance, it would not be a matter of humans leaving Earth with their spaceships for ever, but of leaving Earth "only" until the atmosphere, the lithosphere and the biosphere of Earth had regenerated again. For even if the worst-case scenario of complete annihilation could be brought about by the eruptions of the supervolcanoes, this would not wipe out all life on Earth. But it would certainly take millions of years for the atmosphere, the lithosphere, and the biosphere of Earth to regenerate to such an extent that humans could live on Earth again.

However, in the worst-case scenario, these spaceships, which could be used to evacuate a quantity of humans from Earth necessary for the survival of Mankind, would have to be built in such a way that the humans in the spaceships could survive even if the atmosphere, the biosphere, or the lithosphere of Earth did not recover to such an extent that humans could live on Earth again. Therefore, these spaceships would have to be equipped with a biosphere that would enable the humans in these spaceships to survive forever in these spaceships. They would have to be so-called **generational spaceships**.

A generational spaceship is a hypothetical spacecraft concept designed to explore interstellar space and also enable human settlements on distant planets. The term "generational spaceship" refers to the fact that such spaceships would have to be operated over several generations, as the travel times to other solar systems are very long.

The idea behind a generational spaceship is based on the assumption that the technological challenges and vast distances in interstellar space make it difficult or impossible to send a single crew that could survive the entire journey time. Instead, on a generational spaceship, several successive generations of humans would be born, live and die as they steer the spaceship towards their destination.

Such spaceships would be huge and would, in principle, need to be self-contained ecosystems to ensure the functioning of life support systems, food production, energy supply and other necessities for the crew. The challenges in terms of energy supply, life support and maintaining the mental and physical health of the crew over several generations would be enormous.

In the context of Mankind's survival, however, the concept of the generational spaceship refers not only to possible journeys through interstellar space to other solar systems, but to the survival of Mankind itself in these spaceships. And, as already mentioned, forever.

This "forever" applies, of course, not only because Earth could remain uninhabitable for humans forever due to the eruptions of the supervolcanoes, but also because it would be possible that these humans in their spaceships might also not find another habitable planet on which they could live if they were to embark on an interstellar journey with their spaceships or would then have to embark if Earth were indeed never habitable for humans again in the worst case.

These spaceships for Mankind's journey through interstellar space would of course also have to be designed and built in such a way that they could under no circumstances be destroyed by an event that occurs or could occur in interstellar space. For if they could be destroyed, then the worst-case scenario of complete annihilation could also occur in interstellar space and Mankind would not have survived after all.

This finding can now be generalised in the following way for all events that could occur on the planetary level and that could cause the worst-case scenario of complete annihilation, at least on the planetary level:

a) Humans would have to have developed their technical skills and capabilities to a level that would enable them to prevent these events by whatever means before the occurrence of events that could bring about the worst-case scenario of complete annihilation. Humans would therefore have to be able, in whatever way, to prevent any eruption of a supervolcano or the emergence of large igneous provinces or a devastating pandemic or any other catastrophic event in order to prevent the worst-case scenario of complete annihilation from becoming reality.

b) Before the occurrence of events that could bring about the worst-case scenario of complete annihilation, humans would have to have developed their technical capabilities and possibilities to a level that would enable them to evacuate at least enough humans from Earth to ensure the continued existence of Mankind. According to the current state of technology, this would only be possible in spaceships, which, however, would have to be at an almost unattainably higher technical level than today's spaceships, because they would not only have to be spaceships, but generational spaceships in which, in the worst-case scenario, Mankind could survive forever.

The example of the eruption of the two supervolcanoes has thus shown which preconditions would have to be met in principle for Mankind to survive, at least on the planetary level. But what about the next level, the cosmic level? Do the same conditions for the survival of Mankind apply there as on the planetary level? This depends (of course) on the events that could endanger the survival of Mankind on the cosmic level. So, what are the events that could bring about the worst-case scenario of complete annihilation on the cosmic level?

4.2   The cosmic level

What event surely comes to everyone's mind first when they think of a worst-case scenario of complete annihilation that could be brought about by a cosmic event? Exactly. An asteroid hitting on Earth.

Earth can (of course) indisputably be hit at some point and perhaps only in the distant future by an asteroid that is a planet killer and that annihilates all life on Earth. I will call a "planet killer" or a "global killer" an asteroid that has the potential to cause the worst-case scenario of complete annihilation by its impact on Earth. However, it is also possible that Earth will never be hit by such a planet killer in the future, because it would also indisputably be nothing more than a coincidence if Earth, which is tiny compared to the gigantic dimensions of the universe, were actually to be hit by such an even much tinier asteroid. Nota bene: It is not a question of Earth not being hit by an asteroid at all in the future. Quite the contrary. It will undoubtedly and certainly be the case that Earth will at some point be hit by an asteroid that will cause significant damage to and in Earth's lithosphere, biosphere, and atmosphere, so that millions or even billions of humans will (could) be killed by this impact and by the consequences of this impact. The point is that Earth will be hit by an asteroid that would completely annihilate Mankind through the destructive potential of its impact. However, according to the current state of astronomical knowledge, no asteroid the size of a planet killer can be identified that could be predicted to impact on Earth based on celestial mechanical calculations.

However, this does not change the fact that unlike planetary events, which as individual events almost certainly lack the destructive potential to bring about the worst-case scenario of complete annihilation, a single asteroid impact on Earth may very well have the destructive potential to bring about the end of Mankind and kill all humans by its impact.

The question of what measures the humans should have taken before the impact of such an asteroid in order to prevent this impact or to escape the deadly consequences of this impact can now also be answered relatively easily and the answer is identical to the answer on the planetary level:

a) The humans would have to have developed their technical abilities and possibilities before the impact of such an asteroid in such a way that they would be able to prevent this impact of a planet killer on Earth in whatever way.

At present, there are many theoretically possible but no practically feasible methods to deflect a planet killer (which would have a diameter of at least 30 kilometres) on its way to Earth and thus prevent its impact on Earth. Perhaps this will be possible one day in the rather distant future. At the moment, however, deflecting a planet killer on its way to Earth is not feasible for humans.

If it were not possible to prevent the impact of a planet killer on Earth in the distant future, by whatever method and in whatever way, there would still be another possibility, which has also already been presented:

b) The humans would have to have developed their technical abilities and possibilities to such an extent before the discovery of a planet killer on its way to Earth that, if they were to discover a planet killer on its way to Earth and were unable to prevent the impact on Earth, they would be able to evacuate at least so many humans from Earth that the continued existence of Mankind would be guaranteed despite the impact of the asteroid.

As already mentioned, this is currently only conceivable by humans building spaceships as generational spaceships in which these evacuated humans could survive, at least in the vicinity of Earth, until Earth's biosphere, lithosphere and atmosphere had recovered from the impact of this asteroid to such an extent that humans could repopulate Earth.

If, however, humans take into account the worst-case scenario that could result from an asteroid impact, then, as already mentioned, humans would have to build such generational spaceships on or in which they could survive forever as humans, since on the one hand it would be possible that Earth could never again be habitable for humans as a result of this asteroid impact and, on the other hand, humans would also not find any other place to live on during their journey through interstellar space.

Such an event of an asteroid impact on Earth would, as already mentioned, have a more or less random quality. This is because there is no knowledge of whether Earth could actually be hit by an asteroid in the future that could cause the worst-case scenario of complete annihilation. It could be the case that Mankind is annihilated by the impact of a planet killer on Earth. But it could also not be the case.

On the cosmic level, however, there is an event that has a completely different quality, since the occurrence of this event can be calculated in advance on the basis of scientific and, above all, physical knowledge and thus does not occur more or less by chance and which, if it does occur, would necessarily bring about the worst-case scenario of complete annihilation. This event will necessarily occur under the given physical laws and, if it does occur, it would necessarily mean the end of Mankind.

This event will be brought about by the Sun. For the Sun, with its energy, has not only made possible the emergence of life on Earth. With its energy, it will also destroy all life and thus also all human life on Earth. The reason for this is the way in which energy is generated in the Sun.

As everyone knows, energy generation in stars and thus also in the Sun is based on nuclear fusion.

Nuclear fusion in stars, including the Sun, is essentially based on a process called the pp-chain, in which hydrogen is fused into helium. This process releases enormous amounts of energy that produce the starlight and associated thermal energy.

The amounts of energy converted are enormous (at least by earthly and human standards). The luminosity of the Sun

"is around 385 trillion trillion watts. This means that the Sun loses energy of around 385 trillion trillion joules per second in the form of light. Since the fusion of one kilogram of hydrogen into helium delivers 628 trillion joules of energy, about 600 million tonnes of hydrogen must pass through the pp-chain every second to maintain the Sun's luminosity. This produces about 595 million tonnes of helium. The remainder of about five million tonnes is converted into electromagnetic radiation and radiated from the surface of the Sun" (Lesch/Müller 2023; p. 134).

This process of nuclear fusion and the associated qualitative and quantitative changes in the interior of the Sun over time lead to a gradual increase in the solar constant on Earth.

The **solar constant** is the amount of solar energy that hits Earth's upper atmosphere per unit area perpendicular to the Sun's direction of radiation. It is measured in watts per square metre.

Studies of sedimentary rocks and fossils indicate that the solar constant was about 30 per cent lower than today about 4.5 billion years ago, at the beginning of the solar system. This means that the Sun

"4.5 billion years ago with a luminosity of 2.78 x 1026 watts and a radius of 659,000 kilometres" (Lesch/ Müller 2023; p. 142)

began its life as a star. Today the Sun has

"a luminosity of 3.9 x 1026 watts and its radius has increased to 694,000 kilometres. During this phase of hydrogen burning, which has lasted 4.5 billion years, the Sun's luminosity has increased by 40 per cent and its radius by 5 per cent. Until the end of the hydrogen burning, the Sun will again increase considerably in both luminosity and size" (Lesch/Müller 2023; p. 142).

However, the exact rate at which the solar constant is increasing is the subject of research and debate. An estimate of 1 per cent increase per 100 million years is a common assumption, but there are still uncertainties in this regard, so that further studies are necessary to determine the extent of this increase more precisely. There is no doubt, however, that the solar constant is gradually increasing due to the processes of nuclear fusion taking place inside the Sun.

The steady increase in the solar constant over the course of Earth's history due to the process of nuclear fusion inside the Sun has led and will continue to lead to an increase in the average global temperature on Earth. In about a billion years, the average global temperature will exceed 30 degrees Celsius, reaching a critical level for life on Earth. In about 3 billion years, the average temperature on Earth will be 100 degrees Celsius. The oceans will boil (or have long since boiled away by then) and life in any form will be impossible on Earth.

The increasing warming of Earth due to nuclear fusion inside the Sun is an event that will certainly occur due to the given boundary conditions and the current state of scientific knowledge, especially physical knowledge and laws, and this event will certainly bring about the worst-case scenario of complete annihilation, since it will inevitably heat

Earth to a temperature at which human life on Earth is no longer possible. If Mankind were not able to prevent or evade this event in whatever way, the Sun's energy would certainly annihilate Mankind by that time at the latest.

Thus, even in this case of lethal warming of Earth by the Sun, the preconditions can be stated by which humans would be able to survive the worst-case scenario of complete annihilation by lethal warming of Earth by the Sun. Unsurprisingly, these preconditions are the same as those that would ensure the survival of Mankind already on the planetary scale. The two preconditions are:

1. The humans would have to have developed their technical abilities and possibilities (long) before the deadly warming of Earth by the Sun in such a way that it would be possible for them to prevent this deadly warming of Earth by the Sun in whatever way.

No reasonable statements can be made about this possibility of preventing the end of Mankind through the deadly warming of Earth by the Sun by technical means, since it is currently beyond all human imagination and beyond all human possibilities to influence nuclear fusion within the Sun in whatever way so that this deadly warming of Earth by the Sun would not occur.

However, as with the possibility of a planet killer impacting on Earth, there remains another possibility:

2. The humans would have to have developed their technical abilities and possibilities long before the deadly warming of Earth by the Sun in such a way that then, if the warming of Earth by the Sun would make human life on Earth impossible, at least so many humans from Earth could be evacuated that the continued existence of Mankind would be guaranteed despite the destruction of all life on Earth by the Sun.

To repeat, this is currently only conceivable by humans building spaceships as generational spaceships in which so many humans could survive the deadly warming of Earth that the continued existence of Mankind would be assured.

However, this evacuation of Earth would not be about humans being able to survive on these generational spaceships, at least in the vicinity of Earth, until Earth's biosphere, lithosphere and atmosphere had recovered sufficiently for humans to repopulate Earth. In this case, the destruction of all life on Earth by the Sun would be final and irreversible. For the Sun would not then return to a state that would no longer heat Earth to such an extent that life and also human life would once again be possible on Earth. Quite the contrary. It is even possible that the Sun will completely destroy Earth as a planet.

For the Sun will continue to inflate and increase in radiation intensity through the nuclear fusion processes in its interior even when it has long since burnt up and destroyed all life on Earth through its increase in size and radiation intensity. At the end of its life, it will then have inflated into a so-called **Red Giant**, which will certainly devour and thus destroy the two inner planets Venus and Mercury and perhaps also Earth.

"The question of how the world will end has always been the subject of speculation and discussion among poets and thinkers. Thanks to science, we now know the answer: the world will end in fire. In fire - definitely. In about five billion years, the Sun will swell into a so-called Red Giant, engulf Mercury and perhaps Venus, and turn Earth into a charred, inanimate, magma-covered lump of rock. The dead, smouldering remnant of Earth will also probably be fated to enter the Sun's outer layers and scatter its atoms in the churning atmosphere of the dying star" (Mack 2021; p. 9f).

In the event of an increase in the Sun's radiation intensity, there will be no return for humans to an Earth on which human life could be possible again. Perhaps Earth as a planet will survive the inflation of the Sun into a Red Giant, but it can be assumed that there will be no more water or atmosphere on Earth afterwards, and there never will be again. And life on Earth was destroyed long before that by the increase in the Sun's radiation intensity.

From the events discussed so far that could bring about the worst-case scenario of complete annihilation, one major conclusion can now be drawn:

Mankind could always survive events that could bring about the worst-case scenario of complete annihilation if the humans were able to leave Earth with at least so many humans in a way that the continuation of Mankind would be ensured in the worst case even without Earth. This applies both to events on the planetary level and to events on the cosmic level.

If two supervolcanoes were to erupt on Earth at the same time, as assumed in the above example, because humans would have neither the technical skills nor the technical possibilities to prevent the eruption of supervolcanoes, and if the eruption of these two supervolcanoes would cause the worst-case scenario of complete annihilation, then Mankind could survive if humans could at least leave Earth and survive outside of Earth for what would probably be a very long period of time.

If a planet killer were discovered that was going to hit Earth and humans could not prevent this planet killer from hitting Earth by whatever means, then Mankind could survive if humans could at least leave Earth and survive outside of it for what would probably be a very long period of time.

If humans do not succeed in influencing nuclear fusion inside the Sun in such a way that the Sun will not destroy all life on Earth and Earth as a planet by increasing its size and radiation intensity, then Mankind might survive if humans could leave Earth and survive forever without Earth in the universe.

So, if the humans could find a way to leave Earth and survive without Earth, they could also survive any event that might bring about the worst-case scenario of complete annihilation on the planetary as well as on the cosmic level.

At this point, however, I am not yet at the end of my search for the prerequisites that could guarantee the survival of Mankind under all circumstances and in any case. For the cosmological level is still missing. That is, the level of the universe itself.

The universe is the term I use to describe all the space, matter, energy, and physical laws that exist. The universe encompasses everything that exists. From the smallest subatomic particles to the largest galaxies and all the structures in between.

How would the survival of Mankind now be realised in relation to the universe itself and thus on the cosmological level?

4.3   The cosmological level

To answer this question, I assume that in a distant future humans will have acquired the technical skills and possibilities to build spaceships with which they can leave Earth and with which they can survive forever in space. In order to be prepared for an event that could bring about the worst-case scenario of complete annihilation, the humans have also already built enough of these spaceships and have also determined the criteria on the basis of which humans from Earth are to be evacuated with these spaceships in the event of an eventuality.

Since the humans know that the Sun will inevitably destroy all life on Earth by increasing its size and the intensity of its radiation, they now decide to send the humans intended for evacuation on a journey into interstellar space with the spaceships they have built long before the Sun fatally heats up Earth, in order perhaps to find a new Earth there or to survive forever as Mankind in these spaceships. The part of Mankind remaining on Earth would be annihilated at the latest when the Sun had heated Earth to such an extent that human life on it would no longer be possible.

Would that save Mankind? No, one cannot assume that. For the universe in which the spaceships of Mankind are located with the humans on board is not a static universe but is dynamic and changing. This does not only mean that stars such as the Sun are formed and disappear again, that planets are formed and destroyed again, or that galaxies form clusters of galaxies or merge with each other, just as the Milky Way will merge with the Andromeda Galaxy in the distant future. The universe is dynamic because the universe itself changes in its structure and make-up.

Probably the best-known example of the dynamics of the universe is the observation that the universe is expanding. It is one of the established cosmological findings that the universe is expanding. At least that part of the universe that Mankind can observe. The observation of the expansion of the universe was first made in the 1920s, when astronomer Edwin Hubble discovered that galaxies are moving away from us as observers of the universe. Hubble's observations led to the development of the theory of cosmic expansion.

The expansion of the universe means that the distance between galaxies increases over time. This is not motion in the traditional sense, where objects move through a space. Rather, space itself is expanding, causing objects to move further apart.

An analogy often used to illustrate this process is the idea of dots on the surface of an inflatable ball. When the ball is inflated, the surface expands and the dots move away from each other, although they are not actively moving.

Now, however, it has not only been observed that the universe is expanding, but that it is even expanding at an accelerated rate.

Based on current astronomical, cosmological, and astrophysical observations and findings, most cosmologists believe that the universe is indeed in an accelerated expansion phase.

This accelerated expansion of the universe was surprising because the gravitational effect of matter in the universe had been expected to cause the expansion of the universe to gradually slow down. To explain this accelerated expansion of the universe, the existence of **Dark Energy** was proposed. Dark Energy is a hypothetical form of energy postulated in modern physics and cosmology.

However, Dark Energy is not a conventional form of energy like light or kinetic energy. It is "dark" because it cannot be directly observed or detected in the laboratory. It is a type of energy that could be a property of space itself and has a negative pressure component. This negative pressure component would create a repulsive gravitational effect that accelerates the expansion of the universe.

The existence and properties of Dark Energy are the subject of intense scientific research and debate, but so far this has not led to any findings or insights into what Dark Energy might be.

The discovery of the accelerated expansion of the universe has had a significant impact on cosmologists' ideas about cosmic evolution. The discovery of the accelerated expansion of the universe has also contributed to the idea of the **heat death** of the universe, as the accelerated expansion could lead in the long term to a state in which the universe becomes increasingly empty and colder.

The **heat death** of the universe is a hypothetical idea about the future of the universe based on the idea that the universe is expanding and cooling at an accelerated rate. According to this idea, at some point the universe will be in a state of maximum entropy in which there is no more usable energy and all processes have come to a standstill. This state is called "heat death".

According to the **second law of thermodynamics**, the universe (when considered as an isolated system) tends to go from a state of lower entropy to a state of higher entropy. **Entropy** is a measure of the disorder or chaos in a system. The second law of thermodynamics states that the entropy of an isolated system always increases or remains constant over time, but never decreases. The second law of thermodynamics thus also states in the broadest sense that natural processes of energy transfer and energy conversion in the universe always lead to the entropy of the universe increasing and thus the usable energy in the universe decreasing until the universe is in so-called thermodynamic equilibrium and would thus have died a heat death.

"The entropy is used as a measure of disorder or randomness: the more random a matter distribution, the greater its entropy. We can now formulate the second law of thermodynamics as follows: Every irreversible energy transfer or energy transformation increases the entropy of the universe. Although order may increase locally, there is an inexorable trend towards random arrangement of the matter of the universe as a whole" (Campbell 2021; p. 111).

The fundamental law of the second law of thermodynamics can be illustrated very well using the basic thermodynamic structure of living beings and animals, and it can also be shown that the heat death of the universe would inevitably mean death for all living beings and animals in this universe.

The following quotation briefly and succinctly describes what is meant by a living being and thus also by an animal:

"Living beings are chemical, physical and information-processing machines. They produce their own metabolism with the help of which they keep themselves alive, grow and reproduce. These living machines are coordinated and integrated through the processing of information, with the result that living beings operate as purposeful wholes" (Nurse 2021; p. 165).

Fundamental for all living beings is thus their (own) metabolism, which is the condition for these living beings to remain alive. Living beings and animals need a metabolism because they "operate as purposeful wholes", i.e., they have an inner order and an inner structure which they maintain through their metabolism.

But what is meant by metabolism?

"The totality of the enormous number of chemical reactions that take place in a living organism is called metabolism. It is the basis of all activities of living things - maintenance, growth, organisation, and reproduction - and the energy source of these processes. Metabolism is the chemistry of life" (Nurse 2021; p. 82).

Or, to put it again in other words:

"Metabolism is the totality of the (bio)chemical processes that take place in an organism and serve to build and transform it or to maintain its substance, function and energy supply" (Campbell 2021; p. 110).

However, this inner order and this inner structure of living beings and animals as purposeful wholes seemingly contradicts the second law of thermodynamics, since living beings and animals obviously maintain their inner order and their inner structure against the tendency of the universe towards a random, disordered, and unstructured distribution of matter.

Thus, from the perspective of thermodynamics, living beings and animals are collections of matter that exhibit a non-random order and structure, although this order and structure would spontaneously (i.e., by itself) change into a state of disorder according to the second law of thermodynamics if living beings were not open systems with a metabolism.

"An isolated system, approximately for example the liquid in a thermos flask, can exchange neither matter nor energy with its surroundings. A closed system can exchange energy but no matter with its environment. In an open system, both matter and energy can be exchanged with the environment. Organisms are therefore open systems" (Campbell 2021; p. 111).

According to the second law of thermodynamics, living beings and animals as open systems are in a state of disequilibrium with their environment, since they constantly carry out irreversible energy conversions through their metabolism and would thus sooner or later have to reach a thermodynamic equilibrium with their environment, but can nevertheless maintain their order and structure. Living beings and animals achieve this by being open systems that constantly absorb substances with low entropy from their environment (e.g., other animals), convert the energy contained therein into work for the maintenance of their structure and order and into heat, and release the resulting waste substances and heat back into their environment. Living beings and animals thus stay alive by utilising the (possible) energy gradients in their environment through their metabolism (by digesting other animals, for example). Living beings and animals as open systems can maintain their state of low entropy because they increase the entropy of their environment accordingly through their metabolism and thus do not contradict the second law of thermodynamics.

"In an isolated system, reactions inevitably reach a state of equilibrium in which they can no longer do any work. The chemical reactions of metabolism are irreversible, and they too would reach equilibrium if they took place in isolation in a test tube. Since a system in equilibrium [...] can no longer do any work, a cell that is in chemical equilibrium is simply dead. The fact that the metabolism as a whole is never in equilibrium is the outstanding feature of life. The living cell is an open system which, from a biological point of view, must never reach a state of equilibrium: the constant inflow and outflow of substances prevents the chemical reactions of metabolism from ever reaching equilibrium, and so the cell does work throughout its life. As long as our cells have a continuing supply of glucose, other fuels and oxygen, and can eliminate waste products, the chemical reactions of metabolism never reach equilibrium and so keep the processes of life continually going" (Campbell 2021; p. 114).

Living beings and thus also animals are entropy-generating machines. Life in the form of living beings and also of animals seems to exist in the universe because living beings and animals are highly efficient machines for generating an entropy surplus and thus increasing the total entropy of the universe. It can be assumed that for this reason, whenever there is even the slightest possibility of life arising anywhere in the universe, life will arise.

Living beings and animals thus always need energy gradients in their environment that they can use for their metabolism in order to stay alive and to be able to operate as "purposeful wholes". However, if the universe now expands (at an accelerated rate) and cools down, the entropy of the universe continuously increases and the energy gradients that can be used by living beings and animals decrease more and more, since all structures in the universe dissolve and disappear in the course of time and thus the usable energy stored in these structures also decreases more and more.

"Whether or not the universe can be considered an isolated system is debatable, but if it is considered as such, one comes to the conclusion that the future of the cosmos will inevitably be determined by an increase in disorder and decay. The regularity formulated by the second law of thermodynamics is considered so inevitable and fundamental that it is even held responsible for the passage of time" (Mack 2021; p. 110f).

Even if the humans in their spaceships could avoid all events that could cause the worst-case scenario of complete annihilation on the cosmic level, they would still not be able to avoid the heat death of the universe in this case. And if the future of the universe were heat death, then this would, as one can already guess, have quite unpleasant consequences for the humans in their spaceships.

The heat death of the universe would therefore have quite unpleasant consequences for the humans in their spaceships, because they would still be living beings and animals despite their then highly developed science and technology. They would always have to create and maintain a biosphere for themselves as living beings and animals within their spaceships in which they could live and survive. In order to create and maintain this biosphere, they would necessarily also have to maintain the structure and function of their spaceships. To do this, however, they would, it is assumed, need a lot of energy and thus also a universe that provides a sufficient amount of usable energy gradients for them.

However, it can be deduced from the fundamental laws of thermodynamics that, as already mentioned, in a universe in a state of heat death there would no longer be any usable energy, because there would no longer be any energy gradients. So, if the universe were to die of heat death and enter the state of maximum entropy, then at this point at the latest there would no longer be any energy for the humans in their spaceships to use. The available energy would be reduced to a minimum and no conversion into usable forms such as work, or movement would be possible anymore.

"Energy gradients are the basis of life. But also, of all other structures or machines that do any kind of work. But in a universe that is just one gigantic (very cold) heat bath, there can be no energy gradients. Heat is useless. Heat is death" (Mack 2021; p. 118).

In a universe that has died the heat death, there would be no energy left for the humans to maintain the structure and function of their spaceships, the biosphere within their spaceships and thus also their structure and function as living beings and animals. If the universe dies the heat death, then this event would necessarily bring about the worst-case scenario of complete annihilation and mean the necessary end of Mankind.

However, from the possibility that the universe could die of heat death as a conclusion from the current astrophysical and cosmological findings, one can in turn draw the conclusion that it would be possible that the universe, due to its dynamics and development, could in principle always reach a state that would make life and then also human life impossible in the entire universe. As an alternative to the possibility of heat death, which the universe could realise, the possibilities of the "Big Rip", the "Big Crunch" or also the possibility of vacuum decay are still being discussed, among others. I will not go into these individual possibilities of the development of the universe in more detail, since only the following conclusion from these possible developments of the universe is decisive here: All these possible developments of the universe would lead to the fact that life and thus also human life would no longer be possible in the universe, and through these developments the worst-case scenario of complete annihilation would necessarily occur. What does the cosmologist and astrophysicist say about this?

"I have found no serious thesis in the current cosmological literature that the universe could continue unchanged forever. In the unanimous opinion of all cosmologists, there will at least be a transition that destroys everything and makes at least the observable parts of the cosmos uninhabitable for organised structures" (Mack 2021; p. 22).

With this, one can now formulate the first of two conditions that could guarantee the survival of Mankind on the cosmological level under all circumstances and in any case:

a) The humans would, before the universe in which they currently find themselves would foreseeably develop towards a state that would make life and thus human life in this universe impossible, have to have developed their technical and scientific abilities to such an extent that it would be possible for them to prevent the development of this universe towards this state by whatever means. In other words, the humans would have to be able to control the development of this universe and thus this universe itself in such a way that they could under all circumstances and in any case prevent this universe from reaching a state that would necessarily bring about the worst-case scenario of complete annihilation.

Now, if the humans never succeed in controlling either this or any other universe, another possibility arises which could guarantee the survival of Mankind on the cosmological level under all circumstances and in any case:

b) The humans would, before the universe in which they currently find themselves would foreseeably develop into a state that would make life, and thus also human life, impossible in this universe, have to have developed their technical and scientific abilities to such an extent that they could then evacuate at least so many humans by whatever means from this universe into another universe, which would have to be such that life and thus also human life would be possible in it at least for a certain time, so that the continuation of Mankind would be guaranteed despite the impossibility of all life in the universe from which the humans have fled.

In order for the survival of Mankind to be possible in this case b), there would of course necessarily have to be an infinite number of other universes in the form of parallel universes in addition to the universe in which the humans are in each case, all of which would have to be such that humans could survive in them (at least for a certain time) with (or without) their spaceships.

The term "parallel universe" refers to the idea that there are other universes that exist independently of (and not outside of) the universe known to humans. In a parallel universe, the laws of physics, the constants of nature or the initial conditions could be different, leading to a completely different reality.

The idea of parallel universes is part of some scientific theories discussed in the framework of quantum physics, elementary particle physics, astrophysics, and cosmology. In the course of their development, these theories have also produced and designed various models of reality and the universe according to which parallel universes could exist.

Parallel universes are currently only speculative concepts and there is no direct evidence for their existence. However, since they are derived from certain physical theories, many scientists continue to study this topic and try to develop experimental methods to prove or disprove the existence of parallel universes.

And why would there theoretically have to be an infinite number of these parallel universes so that the worst-case scenario of complete annihilation does not occur in any case and under any circumstances? The simple reason for this is that it could be the case that humans change from this universe to another universe that has the same composition as this universe and in which they could live, but because it has the same composition as this universe, it is also a dynamic universe and through its development could then also reach a state that would make life and thus human life in it impossible. Now, if humans were not able to control this universe into which they have fled and if this universe into which they have fled were in turn to foreseeably evolve into a state that would make life and thus also human life in it impossible, then humans would inevitably have to (be able to) change again into a universe that has the same nature as the universe in which they were able to live before it changed into a state that made life and then also human life in it impossible. And if the humans would never be able to control any universe in which they are at the moment, and possibly any universe in which the humans have taken refuge and in which they are at the moment could, because of its nature, evolve towards a condition which would make life and then also human life in it impossible, then there must necessarily be an infinite number of universes which could initially make the survival of Mankind possible by their nature and into which the humans could then take refuge if the universe in which the humans are currently located were to foreseeably develop into a state which would make life and thus also human life in it impossible. If the future for Mankind, if it is to survive, must be infinite, but every universe that exists would only be habitable for a finite time for humans, then there must be an infinite number of universes that would be habitable for humans, since humans would then have to take refuge an infinite number of times from a universe that would no longer be habitable for them into a universe that is still habitable for them.

With this, one can now summarise and conclude, on the basis of current scientific knowledge about Earth, the cosmos and the universe itself, the conditions that could guarantee, in any case and under all circumstances, that the worst-case scenario of complete annihilation would not occur, and that Mankind would survive. I will call these conditions **"the ultimate conditions for the survival of Mankind"** in the following:

1. Humans would have to be able to control the universe in which they currently find themselves in such a way that this universe does not evolve towards a state that would make life, and thus also human life, impossible in it.

2. If humans were not able to control the universe in which they currently find themselves in such a way that it would not evolve towards a state that would make life and thus human life in it impossible, then humans would have to be able, if it is foreseeable that this universe will evolve towards a state that would make life and thus human life in it impossible, to evacuate so many humans to another universe by whatever means, so that the worst-case scenario of complete annihilation would not occur for these evacuated humans and mankind would survive as a result.

3. This universe into which humans would flee, so that at least for these fled humans the worst-case scenario of complete annihilation would not occur, would of course have to be such that human life would be possible in it, and there would have to be an infinite number of such a universe that is such that human life would be

possible in it, since it could be that humans would always have to be evacuated or flee from the universe in which they are at the moment. It could be that people would always have to evacuate or flee from the universe in which they are at the moment, since each of these universes is possibly dynamic and could thus assume a state that would make life and thus also human life in it impossible. Such an evacuation would have to be infinitely possible at any time in an infinite future, so that the worst-case scenario of complete annihilation would never occur, and the history of Mankind would never end.

Am I now at the end of my reflections? No, of course not. Because I have always conducted the considerations so far under the premise that humans are mortal and must sooner or later suffer their biological death in whatever way. But what would it be like if humans could actually become immortal or were actually immortal? What would it mean for the survival of Mankind if humans were actually immortal? In the next chapter I will try to answer these questions.

5 The immortality of humans

It seems to make sense to me at this point to briefly repeat the various possible forms of immortality of humans that I have already introduced in the introduction:

I have called the idea of transcendent immortality the idea that a human being could live on in some kind of immaterial form beyond his biological death. Under the notion of transcendent immortality, a person's body dies, but his or her soul, spirit, consciousness, or ego exists beyond death, virtually forever. This transcendent immortality, as already stated, is not relevant to the survival of Mankind, because transcendent immortality is a merely imagined immortality of humans who have already died and are dead.

For the survival of Mankind, only that immortality of humans is of importance which I have called inner-worldly immortality. On the one hand, I have called the idea of inner-worldly immortality the idea that humans could realise biological immortality, i.e., stop the ageing process of their bodies and achieve an unlimited regenerative capacity of their bodies. On the other hand, I understand inner-worldly immortality to be what I have called machinic immortality. I have called the idea of a machinic immortality the idea that although a human being's body dies, his soul, spirit, consciousness, or ego could in some way be stored on a non-human material substrate or transferred to this non-human material substrate and humans could in this way attain immortality. Of course, it is debatable whether these machinic immortals would then still belong to Mankind, since, like the specimens of the animal species *Homo sapiens*, they would now no longer have a human body. But I don't want to be petty here and still count these machinic immortals as part of Mankind, since they were once "incarnate" humans.

In all these considerations on the machinic immortality of humans, I now presuppose that one actually knows, or at least could know, what is to be understood by the soul, spirit, consciousness or ego of a human and how one could then "pin down", so to speak, at least one of these immaterial entities for the realisation of inner-worldly machinic immortality and store it on a non-human material substrate.

So, could humans achieve inner-worldly immortality?

I begin with biological immortality. What would have to be the case for a human to achieve inner-worldly biological immortality? Well, in my opinion, two conditions would have to be fulfilled:

a) It should be possible to stop the ageing process of the human body. The human body should be able to regenerate itself completely on an ongoing basis. And not only that. Furthermore, one could also demand that it should also be possible to rejuvenate the human body and restore it to its optimal performance. After all, who would want to attain immortality as an old human being with numerous infirmities?

b) It would have to be guaranteed with absolute certainty that no external event would threaten the life of a human being. In other words, no human should be the victim of disease, accidents, natural disasters, wars, intentional or negligent misconduct of other humans, crimes, or other misfortunes.

It is therefore by no means sufficient for biological immortality to stop the ageing process and ensure the unlimited regenerative capacity of the human body. It would also have to exclude all other possibilities by which a human could die apart from the ageing process. Inner-worldly biological immortality is therefore always only relative. Even the Hydra, i.e., the genus of freshwater polyps (not the monster from Greek mythology), which are often cited as the prime example of an immortal organism, "only" have an average life expectancy of several hundred years. Then, usually, some fatal external event has ended the life of a hydra. Biological immortality does not mean that such an immortal organism cannot die by a fatal external event. An organism would then be immortal in the sense of an endless regenerative capacity (which is not impossible), but could still be destroyed and thus killed at any time by internal as well as external influences.

"The statistical causes of death (under current conditions) are known very precisely. From this - at least under the questionable assumption of unchanged general conditions - one can roughly estimate what the average life expectancy would be if we were no longer getting older and could prevent all related diseases. The result is surprisingly meagre. A first rough calculation yields about 500 to 2000 years - depending on the assumptions used to combat all other diseases as well. After this time, we would have drowned in the bathtub, fallen off the ladder, been shot by our girlfriend or simply left voluntarily." (Welsch 2015; p. 157)

If one wants to make humans biologically immortal inner-worldly, then one must defeat not only one but two deaths. On the one hand, one must defeat death, which I will call **the intrinsic death** of a human being, and which occurs simply because humans are aging. On the other hand, one must also defeat death, which I will call **the extrinsic death** of a human being, and which occurs through fatal external events.

Perhaps in this context, one or the other has already noticed that I have so far occasionally made a distinction between "dying" and "being killed", although a human being is biologically dead at the very end, regardless of whether this human being has died or been killed.

Nevertheless, for good reasons, which I will explain in a moment, I want to make the following distinction between "dying" and "being killed" with regard to the biological death of humans:

a) If a human dies, then I want to use this to refer to the intrinsic (biological) death of a human.

In this context, the term "intrinsic" refers to properties or characteristics that arise or exist from within themselves. It describes properties and characteristics that are inherent to a thing or a person as a thing or person and do not depend on external influences. Intrinsic properties or characteristics are therefore inherent and essential to the object or person in question.

b) If a human is killed, then I want to use this to refer to the extrinsic (biological) death of a human.

The term "extrinsic" refers to properties or characteristics that are caused or determined from outside or by external influences. Extrinsic properties and characteristics depend on external factors and are not directly related to the essence or nature of a thing or person.

But what is the significance and what are the consequences of this distinction between the intrinsic and extrinsic death of humans for the assessment of a possible immortality of humans and thus also for the survival of Mankind?

The life of a human is highly threatened and endangered from the moment of conception. Until birth, the threat is even twofold, since the life of an unborn human is inevitably linked to the life of the mother. Even after birth, his life can be destroyed by a whole arsenal of more or less fatal diseases or serious dysfunctions of his body. But the life of the human once conceived is not only threatened by diseases and possible dysfunctions of the body. External events, i.e., events that are not caused by the human body, such as accidents, natural disasters, crimes, wars, or simply unhealthy behaviour (whether intentional or not) can also lead to the (premature) death of a human being. The life of a human can thus be quite short under adverse circumstances. But what would be the consequences if all this did not happen to a human? What would happen if a human were actually spared all diseases throughout his or her life, if he or she were not affected by any events that could threaten his or her life, if he or she did not engage in any health-damaging behaviour, and if, in addition, he or she always had sufficient good food and clean drinking water available? Nevertheless, with advancing age, the following changes, among others, would become apparent in this human (cf. Welsch 2015; p. 47ff):

a) The efficiency of the heart decreases. Less blood is pumped through the veins.

b) The walls of large arteries thicken and stiffen. This can lead to vascular occlusion.

c) The immune system weakens, and autoimmune diseases increase.

d) The alveoli lose elasticity and functionality. At the same time, the respiratory muscles weaken. The entire respiratory system is strongly affected by ageing.

e) The kidneys shrink and lose efficiency. This leads to a slow reduction in the ability to excrete urine and detoxify the body.

f) Muscle mass is lost, and muscle strength is reduced.

g) The bones degrade and the bone density decreases. The cartilage tissue loses elasticity.

h) The digestive system's ability to absorb vitamins, minerals and trace elements deteriorates.

i) The performance of the working memory decreases. This leads to a reduced ability to concentrate and to being more easily distracted.

j) All sensory organs lose functionality and sensitivity.

In the organism of this human, a death clock is thus ticking inexorably, which at some point will lead to a failure of a vital organ or organ system and thus bring his metabolism to a standstill. This human would therefore inevitably die. However, this would happen even if excellent medical care based on the latest scientific knowledge were added to the whole event. At some point, a vital function of his body would fail, which is irreparable and cannot be restored.

"Organisms age when their organ systems and tissues do not regenerate completely. This in turn is the result of changes at the cellular level. (...) Cellular metabolism changes when the death clock is ticking. It influences and restricts the ability of normal body cells and even stem cells to divide. If tissues are no longer sufficiently re-generated, substances that can no longer be de-graded accumulate, the metabolism derails more and more and entire cell lines perish." (Welsch 2015; p. 46)

This is what I call the intrinsic death of a human. Intrinsic death is the death of a human being that occurs solely because this human being has reached a certain age. Intrinsic death corresponds to what is also often called the "natural death" of a human.

"Talk of >natural death< refers to dying and death as processes inherent in human nature" (Wittwer/Schäfer/Frewer 2010; p. 41).

Even if one assumes that a human is not afflicted by any diseases during his life, that he always receives sufficient food (of excellent quality, of course) and that no external events could threaten and end his life, he will still die one day.

The intrinsic death of a living being and animal is the biological death that occurs because a living being and animal eliminates its ability to keep itself alive through its metabolism over time by itself.

Of course, intensive research is being conducted into the causes of this ageing process and how it can be stopped. In research, ageing has long since become a disease that can possibly be cured. Unfortunately, however, the following must be stated:

"To date, there is no widely accepted theory that could uniformly explain the causes and mechanisms of ageing processes". (Welsch 2015; p. 39)

In this respect, there is also still no "therapy" with which one could overcome the intrinsic death of a human.

Now the only open question is why humans have to suffer intrinsic death. Here is the answer:

"The biological reason for the process of ageing with >natural death< as its conclusion is assumed to be in the mechanism of evolution, since a long continuation of life after reproduction would lead to an aggravation of a lack of space and resources, and slow generational changes would mean too slow an adaptation to changing environmental conditions, both of which would be contrary to the preservation of the species" (Wittwer/Schäfer/Frewer 2010; p. 42).

Living beings and animals die because dying offers a selection advantage with regard to the biological evolution of living beings. Through the death of their specimens, animal species can adapt more quickly to changing environmental conditions, since the specimens of an animal species do not only make room for other specimens of the same animal species when they are killed, i.e. suffer extrinsic death, but "automatically" die off after a certain time, so to speak, and under the boundary condition of limited resources available to an animal species, more specimens of an animal species can be produced and born in the same time, thus increasing the variability and adaptability of an animal species to a changing environment.

The death of living beings is thus on the one hand the result and on the other hand at the same time the motor of biological evolution. Biological evolution only functions properly when living beings die.

"Evolution can only occur when living organisms have three decisive characteristics. First, they must be able to reproduce. Second, they need an inheritance system through which information defining the organism's characteristics is copied and inherited during the reproductive process. Third, the inheritance system must have variability, and this variability must also be inherited during reproduction. This variability is the basis on which natural selection operates. The latter produces from slowly and randomly evolved variants over time the seemingly limitless and ever-changing diversity of life forms that surround us. Moreover, for this process to work properly, the living organism must die. Only in this way is the next generation, which may contain more competitive genetic variants, able to replace their predecessors" (Nurse 2021; p. 65f).

Extrinsic, on the other hand, is what I want to call death when it can in principle be prevented by life-saving measures (by whomsoever by whatever means). People like to complain that in the modern, industrialised, affluent society of the West, death is being suppressed and death is disappearing more and more from the public sphere and the individual consciousness. There is another way of looking at it. One can also understand the process of the development of human civilisation as an attempt to enable more and more humans to die their intrinsic death. This includes not only a steady increase in medical and scientific knowledge, whereby diseases that were considered incurable can now be cured. It also includes all measures of civil protection and disaster control, as well as all means and knowledge to predict, ward off and reduce the consequences of natural disasters, for example. One could perhaps even say that the degree of civilisedness of a society is measured by the abilities of this society to be able to prevent and avoid the extrinsic deaths of humans more and more frequently, and that this society thereby enables its members to be able to die their intrinsic deaths.

Humans who would be biologically immortal, because they would no longer age and their bodies could constantly regenerate, could therefore still suffer extrinsic death, if it were not possible for these biologically immortals in every case and under all circumstances to prevent or evade all events by which they could be killed. They could still suffer extrinsic death precisely because the biologically immortal would also have a body that could be destroyed. Humans who were truly biologically immortal would thus have to be both intrinsically and extrinsically immortal.

Thus, if Mankind were to consist only of biologically immortal humans, the worst-case scenario of complete annihilation could also occur for these biologically immortal humans if they were unable to prevent or evade events that could cause them all to suffer extrinsic death. The Mankind that would consist only of biological immortals would have to fulfil the ultimate conditions for the survival of Mankind just as the Mankind that consists only of biological mortals would have to fulfil the ultimate conditions for the survival of Mankind in order to be able to ensure its survival. Thus, nothing would be gained for the survival of Mankind compared to mortal humans if Mankind were to consist only of biological immortals.

Now, as has already been shown, there are also ideas, apart from biological immortality, that one could transfer what one calls the soul, the consciousness, the spirit or the ego of a human being (and whatever that may be in detail) in whatever way to a non-human material substrate other than the human body, that is, store or cache it in some way on a machine or machinic device so that it could survive the biological death of humans and so that at least that part of a human could also attain immortality.

Assuming that it were actually possible to store the spirit, the soul, the consciousness or the ego of a human being on (or in) such a non-human material substrate, in this case one would only be dealing with a shift in the problem. For now, it would have to be ensured that instead of the biological organism, this non-human material substrate, on which this human would be located as an immaterial existence, so to speak, would not be destroyed.

But this brings us back to the same scenarios that I have already discussed in connection with biological immortality. In this case, too, the machinic immortals would ultimately have to succeed in fulfilling the ultimate conditions for the survival of Mankind, since it cannot be ruled out that any universe could evolve towards a state that would destroy all material substrates in that universe. And that would then also mean the extrinsic death of all machinic immortals. The machinic immortals would then have overcome intrinsic death because they would no longer be living beings or animals, but the non-human material substrate on which they would be could also be destroyed and annihilated by external events and thus also the machinic immortals with this substrate. Here, too, it becomes clear that humans would only be truly (inner-worldly) immortal if they had defeated not only intrinsic death but also extrinsic death, regardless of whether they were biologically or machinically immortal.

If Mankind were to consist only of machinic immortals, the worst-case scenario of complete annihilation could also occur for these machinic immortals, if these machinic immortals did not succeed in preventing or evading events through which they could all suffer extrinsic death. The Mankind that would consist only of machinic immortals would have to fulfil the ultimate conditions for the survival of Mankind just as the Mankind that consists only of biological mortals would have to fulfil the ultimate conditions for the survival of Mankind in order to be able to ensure its survival. Thus, as in the case of the biologically immortal compared to the biologically mortal humans, nothing would be gained for the survival of Mankind if Mankind were to consist only of machinic immortals.

But this brings me to the end of my speculations about the preconditions for the continued existence of the animal species *Homo* sapiens and thus also for the survival of Mankind, and in the next chapter I will once again summarise the results of my speculations and considerations.

6 Summary and concluding remarks

The starting point for my reflections on the preconditions for Mankind's survival was the worst-case scenario of complete annihilation, which (to repeat) states the following:

If there is a possibility that all humans who are alive and who are yet to be born, without exception, must die in whatever way and can be killed, then catastrophic events affecting the entire Earth and all humans could possibly lead to this, that all humans without exception would be killed by the effects of such events, or that the effects of such events would at least kill so many humans that the surviving humans would no longer have the possibility to reproduce in whatever way and thus in this way the history of Mankind would come to an end and Mankind would thus also not have survived.

The conditions that guarantee the survival of Mankind under all circumstances and for every conceivable case, and which could thus prevent the occurrence of this worst-case scenario of complete annihilation under all circumstances and for every conceivable case, I have determined as follows, given the scientific knowledge about Earth, the cosmos, and the universe:

1. Humans would have to have developed their technical abilities and their scientific knowledge

to such an extent that they would be able to control a universe in such a way that it could not assume a state that would make human life or life in it impossible. The universe would therefore always have to be in a state or be kept in a state by humans as representatives of the one entire Mankind, which would at least enable so many humans to remain alive at least until they had reproduced and thereby ensured the continuation and thus the survival of Mankind.

This also applies to humans who would have become intrinsically biologically immortal in whatever way. The biologically immortal would have to be able to control the universe in which they find themselves in such a way that this universe would always be in a state through which their body could not be destroyed and annihilated by external events, because only in this way would they be truly immortal.

The same applies to the machinic immortals. They, too, would have to be able to control the universe in which they find themselves in such a way that this universe would always be in a state by which the non-human material substrate on which they would find themselves could not be destroyed and annihilated by external events, since only in this way would they be truly immortal.

2. Should humans never be able to control a universe, then humans would have to be able to evacuate, by whatever means, at least that many humans into another universe than the universe in which these humans are currently located, since the universe in which these humans are currently living could always be a dynamic universe and thus could always also assume a state through which human life would no longer be possible in this universe. However, this other universe would then have to be such that humans could live in it at least for a certain time and would not be killed, so that the survival of these evacuated humans and thus also the survival of Mankind would be guaranteed. Since, in the worst case, every universe in which humans currently exist and into which they have fled could be a dynamic universe and thus every universe could sooner or later assume a state that would make human life in it impossible, there would have to be an infinite number of universes into which humans could take refuge, since the survival of Mankind presupposes an infinite and never-ending future, and thus in this infinite future, in the worst case, there would also have to be an infinite number of universes which, at least at the moment when humans take refuge in them, would have to be such that human life would be possible in them, even though they might later develop into a state that would make hu-

man life in them impossible. If the future of Mankind, if it is to survive, must be infinite, but every universe that exists would only be habitable for humans for a finite time, then there must be an infinite number of universes that would be habitable for humans, since humans would then have to take refuge infinitely often from a universe that would no longer be habitable for them into a universe that is still habitable for them.

This, in turn, would also apply to inner-worldly immortal humans, since precisely the biological and also the machinic immortality of humans would require an infinite future, through which these immortals could exist infinitely long. For this is precisely what the concept of immortality means, as already mentioned: humans live for all eternity, i.e., in a future that extends into infinity.

Since the biologically immortals would also have a body that could be destroyed, if the universe in which they are located were to foreseeably evolve towards a state that would make life and thus also human life in it impossible and they were unable to prevent this, they too would have to be able to take refuge, infinitely often in the worst case, in another universe in which life and thus human life would still be possible. For every universe in which they are and into which they have fled could be a dynamic universe and could thus assume a state that would make human life in it impossible.

The machinic immortals would also be on a non-human material substrate that could be destroyed. Therefore, if the universe in which they are currently located were to foreseeably develop into a state that could destroy this non-human material substrate and they were unable to prevent this, they too would have to be able to take refuge, infinitely often and in the worst case, in another universe in which this non-human material substrate would not be destroyed (at least temporarily). For all these universes into which the machinic immortals would take refuge could in turn assume a state through which their non-human material substrate, on which they are located, could be destroyed.

But now I leave it to you, that is, to you as the human being who has just read this book and who is reading these lines, to judge whether, on the basis of these preconditions for the survival of Mankind, survival of Mankind might actually be possible (even if perhaps only in a distant future).

Literature references

Bostrom, Nick: Die Zukunft der Menschheit. Berlin: Suhrkamp, 2018.

Campbell, Neil A.: Biologie. München: Pearson, 2021.

Greene, Brian: Bis zum Ende der Zeit. München: Pantheon, 2020.

Henning, Tim: Die Zukunft der Menschheit – soll es uns weiter geben? Berlin: J.B. Metzler, 2022.

Hume, David: An Enquiry Concerning Human Understanding / Eine Untersuchung über den menschlichen Verstand; Englisch/Deutsch. Ditzingen: Reclam, 2016.

Junker, Thomas: Die Evolution des Menschen. München: C.H. Beck, 4. Auflage 2021.

Knoll, Andrew H.: Die kürzeste Geschichte der Erde. München: riva, 2023.

Lesch, Harald/Müller, Jörn: Sterne. München: Bassermann, 2023.

Mack, Katie: Das Ende von allem. München: Piper, 2021.

MacLeod, Norman: Arten sterben. Darmstadt: Theiss, 2016.

Naumann, Thomas/Ilja Bohnet: Das rätselhafte Universum. Stuttgart: Franckh-Kosmos, 2022.

Nurse, Paul: Was ist Leben? Berlin: Aufbau, 2. Auflage 2021.

Plessner, Helmuth: Philosophische Anthropologie. Berlin: Suhrkamp, 2019.

Rahmstorf, Stefan: Klima und Wetter bei 3 Grad mehr. In: Wiegandt, Klaus (Hrsg.): 3 Grad mehr. München: oekom, 2022.

Schäfer, Daniel: Der Tod und die Medizin. Berlin Heidelberg: Springer, 2015.

Schrenk, Friedemann: Die Frühzeit des Menschen. München: C.H. Beck, 6. Auflage 2019.

Smil, Vaclav: Wie die Welt wirklich funktioniert. München: C.H. Beck, 2023.

Ward, Peter/Kirschvink, Joe: Eine neue Geschichte des Lebens. München: Pantheon 2018.

Welsch, Norbert: Leben ohne Tod? Berlin Heidelberg: Springer, 2015.

Wiegandt, Klaus (Hrsg.): 3 Grad mehr. München: oekom, 2022.

Wittwer, Héctor / Schäfer, Daniel / Frewer, Andreas (Hrsg.): Sterben und Tod. Stuttgart: J.B. Metzlersche Verlagsbuchhandlung und Carl Ernst Poeschel, 2010.

Wittwer, Héctor: Philosophie des Todes. Ditzingen: Reclam, 2. Auflage 2020.

All translations of the German quotations in this book were made by the author of this book. Care has always been taken to reproduce the content of the quotations in the translation as accurately and literally as possible.

Zeitfracht Medien GmbH
Ferdinand-Jühlke-Straße 7
99095 Erfurt, Deutschland
produktsicherheit@kolibri360.de